TRAINING AND SHOWING
THE CUTTING HORSE

Training and Showing the Cutting Horse

Lynn Campion

THE LYONS PRESS

First published by Prentice Hall Press, 1990.

Printed in Canada

10 9 8 7 6 5 4 3 2 1

CONTENTS

FOREWORD

It is with great pleasure that I am writing the foreword to this outstanding book on cutting and the cutting horse.

I have had the privilege to have been involved with cutting horses since 1952. The National Cutting Horse Association was only six years old at the time, having been established in 1946.

I have been able to watch and be a part of this great sport almost since its inception. I have seen many changes and watched the development of many outstanding horses and trainers and the many influences each has had on the improvement of the sport. It has also been interesting to see the improvement regarding the quality of the horses that we are riding today as compared to those of forty years ago.

The great cutting horse trainer, and my close friend, Shorty Freeman and I put on many cutting horse clinics in the late 1970s and early '80s for the beginning rider. About this same time, Dick Gaines and Don Parker joined with Shorty and me to put on a Trainers' Seminar each year for four years.

These clinics and seminars produced many outstanding riders and trainers who have gone on to win the NCHA Futurity, The Masters, and many other events, including the Top Ten in the Open and Nonpro.

I mention this because, had we had this book at that time, I would have considered it required reading and an absolute must for every participant involved, whether they were trainers or beginners.

I think this is the most in-depth book that has been written on the sport of cutting, covering everything from the first-time cutting horse rider all the way through to the accomplished cutting horse trainer and showman.

I only wish that Lynn Campion had written it sooner.

Thank you, and good luck at the next cutting.

—Jim Reno
NCHA President
1976–1978, 1986–1989

AUTHOR'S NOTE

The sport of cutting has grown tremendously since I first began competing. Not only has membership in regional and national organizations steadily increased, but interest has been fueled by ESPN and Outdoor Life Network television coverage of the bigger events. Despite the sport's growth, the essentials of training and showing remain the same. For this paperback edition of *Training and Showing the Cutting Horse,* I have only a few additional comments:

• Whether or not you are a member of the National Cutting Horse Association, the NCHA *Trainer's Guide* is a great source for finding trainers in your area. I would recommend seeking the advice and expertise from at least one good trainer listed in this manual. However, and as I stress in the first chapter, make sure that the trainer you decide to work with is professional and fits in with your style of doing things. Otherwise, you will miss out on the enjoyment and advancement of your cutting experience.

• Check out the NCHA's Web site at www.nchacutting.com. This site will give you information about current rule changes (very important), a listing of trainers, upcoming competitions, results, horse pedigrees, statistics, television coverage, etc.

• In addition to watching live or televised events, there are some very good cutting videos available to help you improve your skills. Tack supply stores and cutting horse associations are sources for finding these videos.

• There is a new addition to some of the training pens in our country. Young buffaloes are used, along with cattle, in order to spike interest and expression in a horse. Though these animals require a bit of getting used to, they are equally as fast, if not faster, than yearling cattle. But they have different requirements and needs. My advice here is to seek out information about buffaloes from the professionals who mix them with their cattle. I don't recommend buffaloes for green horses or inexperienced handlers.

• Due to the popularity of this sport, a greater variety of horses are used for cutting. Sore backs caused by saddles not built for these conformational differences are now commonplace. And as you may suspect, a horse with a sore back will not work to his ability. Custom saddles and air-filled saddle pads for hard-to-fit horses are available through many tack stores. Also, there are additional therapies that address specific problems: acupuncture, chiropractic work, and water and laser therapy. Ask your vet for more information that can help your horse be the best cutter he can be.

That's it. Enjoy this challenge of working with yourself, your horses, the variety of cattle, terrain, helpers, judges, and the way each day progresses. Then add a little bit of luck into the equation, and you've got the ultimate challenge of cutting a cow and keeping it separated from the herd. There's nothing like it.

—Lynn Campion
July 2000

INTRODUCTION

In the spring of 1984, I stood in the middle of an arena full of people, brushing the dirt off my cowboy hat while half-heartedly waiting to hear my score. It doesn't look good when you lose your hat riding a first-rate cutting horse and working a tough cow, especially during a competition. And in my case, the reason it happened was going to be obvious to everyone watching. My upper body had simply lurched to the right while my horse was pivoting to the left. I was unable to stay in sync with his quick movement. I had a pretty good idea that I needed to go home, lick my wounds, and figure out how to improve my riding.

Years later, I'm still at it. My hat flies off only in a windstorm now, and my technique has improved, as has my ability to "read" cattle. I plan to continue on this roller coaster until I'm one of the oldest riders in NCHA competition. I may need some help getting on my horse once in a while, but after that, I'll still be having fun.

This book is a direct result of losing my hat. It is about the world of the cutting horse, a magnificent animal bred for his instinct and ability to counter the movements of a cow and prevent her return to the herd. This book is for anyone interested in horses and in the cutting horse industry. The beginning cutter can learn how to become involved in cutting, how to ride and train a "green-broke" horse, and how to begin riding in competition. More experienced riders can improve their horsemanship, explore the various training methods used in the country, and learn how to compete. Nonprofessionals can focus on training for competition, and apply the principles of showmanship and psychology toward winning. I hope that pros can learn something too.

I have written about training and showing a cutting horse from my own viewpoint as a nonprofessional rider. This book compiles and organizes the results of five years of asking questions. I've attempted to write down information that many talented, professional trainers can not or will not take the time to write. My experience is not as vast as I would like it to be in order to provide the reader with a full menu of training methods and techniques for successful showing. Yet I've been guided by the expertise of many qualified riders in my search to improve since I took the first of many small blows to my ego, scoring a low mark of 64 and getting my hat dirty.

After many years away from horses and competition, I began my cutting career in 1984 in Idaho. The idea of separating and then holding a cow away from a herd for a certain period of time sounded like a real challenge. I learned all I could about this fast-growing sport from a friend who was a trainer. He helped me buy my first cutting horse, taught me to ride correctly, and then launched me into local competition to get some experience. Since that time, I have competed throughout the Rocky Mountain and West Coast regions, winning championships on both the state and national levels. I've been fortunate—at times. The word *challenge* has become an understatement.

Many, many people have helped me with all aspects of cutting: technique, training, showing, psychology, reading cattle, and reading my horse. Yet I am still a relative beginner in this highly competitive world. I hope this book will stimulate other people, more qualified than I, to write on the same subject.

Most helpful to me in offering ideas and suggestions for the book, as well as in sharing their own approaches to training and showing, were Chubby Turner, Lindy Burch, Mike Haack, Bill Freeman, Joe Heim, and one of the founders of cutting competition, Buster Welch. I would like to thank them. Without their encouragement and positive outlook toward helping others improve, I could not have written about such a technical and psychological sport.

All of the professionals I've mentioned are students of the game. They respect the origins of cow cutting, when it was an important part of a cowboy's existence on ranches in the 1800s. And they work hard to keep the tradition and spirit alive today. They are, however, only a very small portion of the many talented trainers whose ideas I would like to include in a book. There is much for me to learn, and I hope someday to do justice to all of the people who have made cutting what it is today.

Last, I wish to thank the many other trainers and nonpros who have contributed their time and insight. Idaho, though small, has an energetic foothold in the cutting horse industry. There are many pros and nonpros in this state and the adjoining states who helped me formulate my ideas. Their help led directly to my success in competition. Their names are too numerous to mention, but without them my love for this sport would not have grown as it has.

1

MAKING

THE

COMMITMENT

The cutting industry has become a big business in the past ten years and now demands a heavier financial commitment by both owners and riders. As a result of this tremendous growth, investing in a cutting horse merits careful planning with open eyes and a positive attitude. In order to achieve the many rewards that accompany this sport, you'll need to start out with a good foundation. Learn all you can and realistically figure out where you will fit in before you put your money on the line.

Degree of Commitment

Below are a few questions that you should consider before you purchase a cutting horse:

- How involved do you want to be in the cutting horse business? Do you intend to build a full-scale training and breeding operation with complete facilities, or do you simply want to get your feet wet?
- Do you want to ride? Not everyone involved in this sport actually rides a cutting horse. Some people are strictly breeders or investors, or horse-lovers who hire professional trainers to train and ride their horses. For the most part, however, cutting horse enthusiasts seem to wind up in the saddle, even if it's only part time.
- If you would like to ride and compete, how much time can you devote to cutting, and how far do you want to go with it? Everyone has his own set of demands, whether it includes a job, family, or school, and these are important considerations when choosing a horse. If you want to keep a fairly low profile in this sport you can attend local competitions on the weekends that are usually, a lot of fun. But if your sights are set on going to bigger competitions, you must expect to dedicate many hours in the saddle (three to five days per week), to drive all over the country, and to spend a week or two at each show you attend.
- Will you be able to ride year round? If you cannot ride at least three or four days every week, find someone who can keep your horse in shape. Less frequent riding has its disadvantages however, as you can easily forget the "feel" of your horse, as well as lose your timing.

> I live in snow country, where I wrestle with the problem of doing enough riding every winter. There are very few indoor riding facilities in my area, and of those, only two are designed for training cutting horses. As a result of this, I send my younger horses to a trainer in another area and I give the older ones a few months vacation while I ski and write—and lose my timing. In the spring I really have to buckle down and try to make up for time out of the saddle.

- Do you have the funds and the facilities for training horses and keeping cattle or goats? (Goats are also used for practice in some parts of the country.) There's no getting around the fact that cutting is an expensive sport. You certainly don't need to own a lot of land with top facilities, but there are minimum requirements. When investing somewhere between 500 and 1 million dollars on a cutting horse prospect, you want him* to be in a good stall, or a covered pen, with a run so that he's safe from other horses. You should keep him in top condition with nourishing feed, a good health care program, exercise, and shoeing. Also, your cattle need a stout pen of some sort, as well as adequate feed and vetting. And for training, you should have at least one large enclosure with good footing (often a mix of blow sand, soil, and manure).

- Is there a reputable trainer nearby, or will you need to travel far to get help when it's needed?
- If you would like to ride your horse, but still keep him with a trainer, how many days per week could you ride? It is important to discuss this point with your trainer. Each trainer will have his own particular feelings regarding the frequency of lessons. As a rule of thumb, if you are a novice rider and have bought a pretty solid horse (at least four years or older), most trainers will encourage you to ride for an hour or two at least twice a week, so you can learn good habits. However, if the horse is younger and possibly a good cutting prospect, the trainer may feel that you should not ride him often, if at all. Colts in the beginning stages of learning are easily confused by different riders, and especially by novice riders.

Learn about the Cutting Industry

The National Cutting Horse Association is a nonprofit organization consisting of more than 13,000 members and 117 affiliates in the United States, Canada, Australia, South America, New Zealand, Central America, Mexico, and Western Europe. They sanction most of the cutting events held in the United States and abroad, and they keep statistics and financial records on every horse and rider entered in an NCHA sponsored show. Contact them regarding any questions you might have about the industry:

The National Cutting Horse Association
4704 Highway 377 South
Fort Worth, Texas 76116
(817) 244-6188, Web site: www.nchacutting.com

*In order to keep things consistent, I will refer to riders as "he," to horses as "colts" or "he," and to cattle as "cows" or "she." This is an arbitrary classification because there are three gender types which can be used for cattle or horses, and endless confusion would result without such a system.

As a member of the NCHA you will receive:

- The official NCHA *Rule Book*, a very concise manual containing present NCHA rules and regulations, as well as rules for judging and pointers on judging and showing the cutting horse. It is revised and updated yearly.
- The NCHA *Casebook*, designed to explain the rules and to clarify situations that are likely to arise during competition.
- A comprehensive monthly magazine called *Cuttin' Hoss Chatter*, which keeps readers up to date on what's happening around the country. Included are many cutting-related articles as well as a full array of quality advertisements for tack supplies, trainers, horses, breedings, and yearling and dispersement sales.
- The NCHA *Annual Yearbook* lists the present board of directors as well as the top horses and riders from 1946 to the present, NCHA awards, and the names and addresses of all members and affiliate organizations.

Watch Cutting Competitions

There is no better way to learn about cutting than by observation, so try to attend some local and national competitions. Don't be afraid to ask questions; almost every person involved in cutting will welcome a new face. Even the country's top riders are real students of the sport, devoting much of each day to observing and learning from other riders, and sharing ideas.

Find the Right Trainer

Good advice teamed with experience is extremely important when it comes to finding someone who can help you learn or refine your skills. And everyone, even the pro, is constantly seeking to learn more in this business. If you want the help of a professional, look for someone who can best fit your needs and those of your horse. Learn who the good trainers are by asking nonpro riders at any of the regional or national cuttings. They will always have a few names for you to check out. Then, consider the following:

1. Is the location of the trainer important to you? If you are going to be riding your horse during the time he's in training, it makes sense to be within reasonable driving distance of the facilities. But there are many

people who send their horses to be trained in another state for a few months, bringing them back home just before their show season begins.

2. Does the trainer have a good reputation and is he respected in the cutting world? Does he have references whom you can check? Customers of a particular trainer may have some very definite ideas about his strengths and weaknesses that can help you in making your decision. For example, you may hear of one trainer who takes an infinite amount of time with each horse, making sure he has a finished, saleable product that can be ridden easily by a nonpro. Conversely, you might learn that a certain trainer is interested only in prospects that can win, apparently spending little time with the other horses in training.

3. Is his record good? One trainer may not be a showman, but he can produce high-quality cutting horses, while another might be known for his abilities to win in competition. Again, the choice involves your own personal preference: What is important to you and who best can help?

4. Does he train his own horses as well as those of his customers? If so, will he put as much energy into working with your horse on a daily basis? Again, asking other nonpros about this person may help answer this question.

5. How many horses are in his barn and who else rides them? Are the other riders experienced? Most pros have someone who warms up horses and occasionally schools them in training. This is fine as long as you understand the situation and agree with it.

6. Can he train a horse that a nonpro will be able to ride and compete on? This is an important question, for there are many "finished" or fully trained cutting horses which are almost too sensitive and finely tuned for the average nonpro. If you wish to compete on your horse, then your trainer should try to adapt his techniques to the way you ride.

7. Aside from normal training fees (which at this writing range from 400 to 1,200 dollars per month), what are the added costs you'll be expected to pay the trainer for transportation, showing, and other aspects of training? What percentage of the winnings does he receive?

8. Lastly, do you feel comfortable with this trainer or will you be intimidated by him? The key to progress, and to your continuing enthusiasm for the sport, rests in your own attitude and desire. Find someone with whom you can communicate, who will encourage you to move beyond your own perceived limits, and who genuinely likes what he's doing.

Your Own Training Facilities

There are basically three areas that can be used to train cutting horses: a pasture, a large oval or round pen, and a square pen. Having all of these would be ideal but is by no means a necessity, for you can certainly make do with one enclosure if it is large enough.

Good footing is a necessity, no matter where you train. A cutting horse cannot function at 100 percent if his legs or hooves are bruised or injured, so you'll want to do everything in your power to prevent these problems. If you have soil which packs down and becomes too hard, mix in enough blow sand and cow manure so as to have about 3 inches of loose ground over a firm base. If your loose footing is much deeper, however, a horse can strain tendons or be frightened if he should slide too far when attempting a hard stop. Avoid bruised hooves by removing any rocks from your arena, and keep everyone's lungs healthy by watering down a dusty pen before working in it.

Well-known cattleman and trainer Dale Wilkinson has said that the most important thing someone can do for a horse is to train on good ground.

Pasture

If you are lucky enough to have a few acres of good pastureland, or a big open area that is free of holes and rocks, you'll be able to teach your colt a lot about cattle in a natural, unpressured environment. This is also a perfect area to relax and free up the mind of an older, finished cutting horse.

Pens

Most pens are built of wooden posts and rails or with portable metal panels. They often have sheets of plywood tacked up all the way around to form a solid-looking enclosure so that a horse can better concentrate on the job at hand instead of looking at his buddies over in the next field. Also, solid sides prevent a cow from constantly sticking her head through the rails, looking for escape. The net result will be more eye-to-eye contact between horse and cow, an important part of training.

- *A round or oval pen, having a diameter of 120 to 200 feet.* Cutting horses are frequently taken through their entire training program in one or two large circular pens. With gates spaced around the sides, these areas can be used in many ways without creating undue pressure on either a horse or cattle. To increase the versatility even more, some panels can be moved around to allow a horse to work in line against a straight fence.

> Trainer Bill Freeman likes to start a colt in a 120-foot pen, go to a larger one where a horse can learn to move with some speed, then move to a square pen before finishing up training back in the 120-foot pen.

- *An arena 100 feet wide and at least 120 feet long.* If you have ample space for an arena, a square pen can be just as good for training as a large oval pen. With gates in the middle of each side, one can use the length, width, and circumference for training horses of all ages. And, with a few extra panels, the pen can easily be made into an oval or semicircle.

> Chubby Turner trains his horses in an arena at least 100 by 120 feet with gates in every side. He feels that cattle last longer because they aren't as pressured in a larger area, and he likes the many ways it can be used.

Animals Used for Training

Without access to cattle or goats, training a cutting horse is next to impossible. He must learn to "read" and react to another animal in order to counter its movements, and these two herd-oriented species provide him with the challenge he needs. Determine what is available in your area, what the going prices are, and how many animals you can accommodate at one time. You should have a minimum of five or six per horse to work each week. The ideal number would be around fifteen head.

Cattle

Depending upon the market, cattle bring anywhere from sixty-five cents to one dollar per pound. If they are available in your area and can be leased or bought at a reasonable price, consider yourself lucky.

> The cutting horse grew to fame because of his innate ability to work cattle. He is an important part of our western heritage. Although this highly trained athlete will work almost any moving object placed in front of him, I honestly feel I would no longer enjoy the sport of cutting if I couldn't train my horse on cattle.

What to buy. For most riders, the ideal situation would be to have twenty to thirty head of high-quality 500-pound heifers or steers. Called "light" cattle, these healthy yearlings of almost any breed or mix will have fairly good staying power when treated well. They need adequate feed, shelter, rest, and changes in routine; the longer you can keep them "fresh" and respecting your colt, the more days you'll be able to work them without needing to buy replacements.

There are general behavior patterns associated with each breed and crossbreed of cattle, and it's a good idea to become familiar with as many types as possible. You'll find that certain breeds will be more aggressive, and others will be "soft." Some types work well for only three or four turns before becoming crazed and impossible, while others hold up longer. Try to lease or buy different breeds and crosses of cattle during the year so that you can learn about their differences while training. If that isn't feasible, many cutting competitions offer two- to five-minute practice sessions on their "used" cattle.

> There's a certain caution associated with forming set opinions about particular breeds of cattle, however. Just as soon as you think you've figured out which type is best, you'll spend $10,000 to bring home a bunch only to find half of them are duds. This can also be true during competition. You may zero in on the Brahma-crosses, while your fellow competitor earns a higher score using a black baldy, a Holstein, and a Hereford. Knowing the characteristics of each breed will help, but knowing which cow will work the best for your horse is one of the biggest challenges that cutting has to offer.

How to buy cattle. Unless you're lucky enough to own a feedlot or a cattle ranch, fresh cattle of any type or size are fairly hard to come by. Many cutters scramble to come up with cattle every week or two. Here are ways they do it:

- If there is a feedlot nearby, you may be able to work out a deal with the owner. Offer to feed and care for his cattle using his particular feed program. This may require some sort of agreement wherein you guarantee weight gain for those cattle. Another possibility is to offer to lease them, exchanging them every few weeks.

- If there is a county saleyard, you can buy the number of cattle you need, feed them well, and then return them in a few weeks with the chance of making a little money. For those people who have pastureland available, a good method is to buy light 400-pound calves, work half of them for a week or two, turn them out to gain weight and rest while the others are worked, and then rotate them again. This helps to avoid weekly trips to the saleyard.
- A rancher or dairyman will sometimes deal with you, especially if he is familiar with cutting and knows that you won't run his cattle to death. This is a common belief among cattlemen, and although inaccurate, it may take some persuasion to alter their views. Offer to feed and care for his cows in exchange for using them. One or two experiences will show him that cattle calm down and gain weight when kept by a responsible cutter.

Goats

With cattle prices high, goats are a good alternative for use in training a cutting horse. They have similarities to cattle in the way they work, and they like to stay grouped together. Goats are said to last a little longer than cattle because of their temperament.

Be warned: Goats are the animal version of Houdini. If you can't provide an escape-proof enclosure or a high-fenced arena, they won't be around for long.

2

CHOOSING

THE

RIGHT

HORSE

Picking out a cutting horse prospect, though always a bit of a gamble, requires investigation, good sense, and sound judgment. You should learn about the various bloodlines and crosses that are producing winners; the more research you do the better your odds of finding the right horse. If you've figured out your budget, decided whether and for how long you will need a trainer, and determined what your goals are, the next step is to consider the type of horse that will fit your needs. Know whether you want to buy for learning, competition, breeding, or resale. Then find a qualified person to help you, someone who has your best interests at heart. Cutting, which offers so much in the way of challenge and reward, will be considerably more fun if you get started on the right horse.

Several breeds of horses will readily learn to cut cattle. Quarter horses or quarter horse–thoroughbred crosses are probably the most popular. But Arabians, paints, Appaloosas, and mixed breeds can hold their own in cutting and competition.

As far as the best age and gender of horse to look for, many trainers (Joe Heim is a good example) would advise a nonpro to buy a mare or gelding at *least* four years old. Stallions can be unpredictable because of their more aggressive temperament. Younger horses are still in the basic stages of learning where they can easily pick up on the mistakes of an inexperienced rider. If you are a beginning cutter, consider purchasing a more mature and well-trained horse to start out on, one that has already seen plenty of competition. This type of horse will help you learn how to read cattle. Because he is experienced and won't require constant correcting, you'll have time to focus your attention on your own skills without having to worry about correcting or ruining the horse.

No matter what your level of expertise, don't lose sight of the fact that you are entering this sport for fun and challenge. Defeat comes rapidly to those who think they can tough it out by buying and riding a horse that is above (or below) their own particular ability levels.

Age and Cost

However you look at it, a good cutting horse is going to be expensive. This can mean anywhere from 7,000 dollars up to a few million. After the initial purchase come other costs, in addition to stabling, feed, vetting, and training that were mentioned earlier. Competition expenses (which include transportation, motel, stalls, and entry fees) add up fast, especially if you had an unlucky day or are riding a horse you're not suited to. So think things out before putting your money on the table, and get advice from someone who's looking after your best interests. A horse that's good for your friend might not necessarily be the right one for you.

Yearlings

If you have another horse to ride, and don't mind waiting the extra twelve months for his mind and body to develop to a trainable age, a well-bred yearling can be a smart investment. Its bloodlines are going to be your only real indication of his future, but if you have the facilities to keep him for a year and a good person to start him, he may well be worth a try.

When looking at a yearling prospect, watch the way he moves in an open environment, such as a big pen or pasture. He should have a natural gait, good hock action, straight legs, and no obvious defects. He should be healthy looking, with a glossy coat and watchful eye. Ask questions about each prospect that you look over: Is he broke to lead, to load in a trailer, to stand quietly while being brushed? Does he have any problems you should be aware of? Have his wolf teeth been removed? Has he had a good worming and vaccination program? What type of hay and supplement does he get?

If the yearling has a good pedigree, find out whether he is eligible for any special cutting events that could add to his worth. The offspring of many of the more well-known studs are often eligible to compete in cuttings that are solely open to them.

Two-Year-Olds

A two-year-old, especially one that has already been started in training, will be more expensive than a yearling, but worth the investment if you want to compete in the three-year-old futurities. At this age, you can get a better idea of his temperament, build, and natural way of moving. And if his bloodlines have been producing winners, he has everything going for him. In addition to the points mentioned earlier, you'll want to know whether the colt has been broken and started on cattle, and who did the initial training.

If you're unsure of riding the colt yourself, ask someone else to ride him while you watch. And if it's possible, ask a pro or an accomplished rider to help you in your decision. All during this process, keep in mind the goals you wish to achieve. Many young cutting horses are ridden by a pro through at least their three-year-old season, especially if the owner-rider is still learning. This helps to cement a good foundation and can pay off handsomely later on.

Limited Age Event Horses

Certain NCHA competitions are limited to horses between the ages of three and six years. Although these youngsters are not nearly as consistent as older horses, the prize money offered in the Aged Events is often quite high. If you have some experience under your belt and want to put the finishing touches on a young horse, or if you have a trainer to help, buying a three-year-old just before the big futurities in the fall can be an excellent investment. There are always good horses for sale in the late summer. The basic training has been done, and the horses have no money against them (meaning that they have no record of winnings and are thus qualified to enter any cutting event).

A four-, five-, or six-year-old with good bloodlines and a good futurity record can be expensive. Ranging in price from 15,000 dollars upwards, these horses have had a minimum of two years of training and will often be quite well broke to cut cattle. There are always bargains to find, however, and they can be well worth searching for with the help of a knowledgeable person. Here again, spend time looking carefully into a horse's background before you let emotion persuade you to buy.

> A typical mistake made by a less experienced nonpro is to spend a lot of money investing in a horse that is far above his level of ability. Unless the animal is ridden three or four times a week by a trainer, his performance level will be only as good as his rider's.

Older Horses

From seven years on up, horses with more experience and time showing in competition will vary greatly in price, depending on their records and their owners' reasons for selling. Look carefully into such a horse's history: How much money has he won in approved NCHA shows? What classes would you be eligible to ride him in? Does he have any physical problems? What is his temperament like? Where has he been, who has trained him, and what type of ground has he been trained on?

> The best advice I got when I began my cutting career came from an Idaho friend and trainer named Dan Manning. Dan helped me buy my first cutting horse—an older, well-broke, black gelding named "Cow Q Later." This horse knew the ropes, he had a good mind, and he liked to work cattle. The result was that I learned the "feel" of a good horse, and I could concentrate on my own riding instead of having to worry about what he was doing. With Dan's good eye and guidance, I was able to get a good foundation and win a few state titles in my first year.

The Backyard Find

And then there's the "backyard find," a horse without proven bloodlines, registration papers, or cutting record. The initial investment may be small, but the gamble is going to be large. Purchasing such a horse is not a very wise choice if you're an inexperienced horseman, for more often than not you'll pour money, time, and a good deal of effort into a horse that has neither the physical ability nor interest in working cattle.

> Speaking of a gamble that paid off, the 1984 and 1985 NCHA World Champion Cutting Horse, Ball O'Flash, did not have registration papers.

Looking Over a
Horse for Purchase

If you're the least bit unsure of yourself when looking at a prospect, ask your trainer or another knowledgeable person to help. Another pair of eyes and a respected opinion can save you lots of money. If you are new to the sport, go to a few of the cuttings and ask several riders who they feel is competent and could help you. Not only do you as a novice need to find someone *qualified* to help, but you must trust that he has *your* best interests at heart instead of those of the seller. In other words, do your homework.

When you've found a reliable person to accompany you when looking at a prospect, the next step is to time your visit so that you see the horse before he's ready to be shown and to work a cow. Look him over when he is in his stall or pen so that you'll be aware of any bad habits he might have. Weaving back and forth, cribbing, pacing, or windsucking might be problems you don't want to deal with. Ask the owner if you can go into the stall to check the horse over. Does the colt want to bite or kick? Is he nervous with people around? Then, watch the whole process of grooming and saddling.

When your prospect is being warmed up, notice how he responds to the rider when he is fresh and feeling good. And as he works a cow, try to figure out what his good and bad habits are, and how they will affect his training. Your trainer will know whether this prospect has been pushed too hard, which is always a possibility, or if he fits your requirements. He'll also be able to tell whether the person riding (especially if it's a pro) is making the horse look better than the animal really is.

> I like to look for style in the way a horse moves. Expression, too. I want to feel that a horse is interested in what he's doing out there in the arena or warm-up pen. I also want to see him bending his hocks easily as he gets "underneath himself" during his stops and turns.

Conformation

Good cutting horses come in all shapes and sizes, but there are a few conformation points to note when searching for a prospect. Basically, you're looking for an athlete: somewhere between fourteen and fifteen hands tall, balanced and agile, fairly narrow in the shoulder between the front legs, and not muscle-bound. Above all, it's preferable that he has good, straight legs, short cannon bones, and a good bend in the hocks. Any obvious defects in the legs, such as lumps or scars, should be a red flag to the prospective buyer and merit further examination by a veterinarian.

Vetting

Before you buy any horse, ask a reputable veterinarian to do a *thorough* health check. He may find defects that are not obvious to you but that could influence your decision to purchase the animal. If your own vet is nearby, ask him to do the examination, for you'll feel confident that he's going to be looking after your best interests. More often than not, however, you'll be in another part of the country, using either the seller's vet or one you otherwise don't know. This should rarely be a problem, for almost everyone involved in the veterinary profession will be honest with you.

Though optional, X rays of lower legs and feet are wise to have, especially when you're buying an expensive horse or one that the vet finds to be sensitive or stiff. An older horse with some miles on him should definitely be X-rayed to rule out problems that come with age. These will cost extra money, but think of it as cheap insurance (once you've bought the horse, he's your responsibility, sound or unsound).

> It's a good idea to agree ahead of time who will pay for the vet exam, as this practice differs around the country. Where I live, a seller who represents his horse as faultless will pay the vet fee if any defects are found and the sale is jeopardized. Otherwise, the vet bill goes to the buyer.

Insurance

Equine insurance is costly, but if you purchase an expensive animal, it's worth it. Some horses can live their entire lives without a problem, but others may as well take up permanent residence at the vet's facility. Learn about the different possibilities for insuring your horse so that you can make your own decision about whether to spend the money.

> I have two opposing comments about insurance. I bought insurance three years ago for one of my horses, and he hasn't even had a cough since the day the policy came through. But I also insured a yearling filly that was in training in California for a few months. She died in a fire—and she was underinsured.

Again, take your time when looking for the right horse to buy. Keep your eyes open and your pocketbook closed until a good prospect comes along; the right price, age, looks, temperament, and ability aren't always going to jell. And a horse that suits one person may not be at all right for another. The best you can do is to be knowledgeable and to recognize what you need in order to make your cutting career a success.

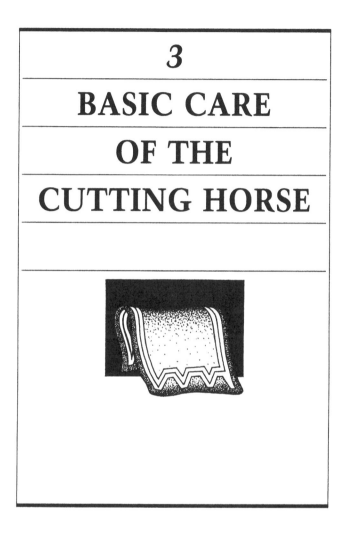

3

BASIC CARE

OF THE

CUTTING HORSE

Proper care of a cutting horse is the mark of a good horseman. Because your horse is an athlete, he should be kept in top mental and physical health. He needs the basics of a good enclosure where he can relax and rest, he needs to be fed correctly, groomed and exercised regularly, and he needs to be part of a good vetting program. This brief chapter is included for those who may not be fully aware of the basic requirements.

Stalls

Most cutting horses are kept in stalls or covered runs. A stall should assure safety and adequate room in which a horse can relax. Measuring 12 by 12 feet or larger, it needs to be solid and free from protruding objects (if there's something around to get hurt on or to kick loose, a horse always finds it). The floor can be of dirt, sand, asphalt, or wood planking. Cottonwood is the best wood to use because it doesn't splinter and it lasts indefinitely. Hard floors should be covered by thick rubber mats that act as insulation and prevent a horse from slipping.

> I like a stall with dutch doors and, if possible, a window on one side to let in more light; horses are sociable animals and like to see what's going on. There's something quite special about walking down the aisle of a barn filled with horses hanging their heads over the stall doors and watching the goings-on.

Bedding

Whether you use straw, shavings, or sawdust on the floor, be sure to provide an adequate amount so that your horse is comfortable when lying down. Replace the soiled bedding daily to avoid urine and manure buildup.

Runs

If you have the space, build outruns for each stall so that your cutting horses can move around in an unpressured environment. Mike Haack says he likes to keep his horses in partially covered 15 by 50 foot runs so that they can loosen up, relax, and be outside in the fresh air.

If you keep your horse in a stall without a run, be sure that he gets at least an hour of daily exercise even if it means simply being let out to run in your arena. Horses in good condition need plenty of exercise and play time.

Water

A horse in training can consume about twelve gallons of water a day. Although automatic waterers are convenient, buckets are sometimes preferred because of the ease in monitoring a horse's water intake. An untouched bucket of water can signal dehydration and sickness. Also, a horse that is already familiar with buckets is more likely to drink a normal amount of water when you are on the road or at a show.

Manger

Feed, salt, and supplements should be kept in a manger or bin that is free of ground dust, sand, and manure.

Feed

Proper nutrition is essential for an athlete. Your cutting horse requires the right balance of carbohydrates, vitamins, minerals, and protein to stay in top condition. Many people use a high-quality alfalfa because it contains more vitamins and minerals than other hays. But other types of hay, and mixes of hay, will also provide excellent results. Of key importance here is that you protect your horse's lungs and digestive system by making certain that his hay is green and fresh-looking, that it smells good, is void of dust or mold, and is relatively free of weeds and stems.

> If you are in doubt about the quality of your hay, ask a county agent to test it. If it's lacking in something, he will then be able to suggest which supplements should be added to create a good balance. The area where I live, for example, has wonderful alfalfa and timothy, but both are low in selenium. I feed a 60/40 combination of these two hays and add a high selenium supplement.

Most cutting horses are fed a certain amount of whole or processed oats on a daily basis, with the addition of cracked corn or sorghum during colder weather. Though not a good source of vitamins, oats are fairly high in protein and energy and they are quite digestible. Be sure to talk with your veterinarian about the amount and type of grain to feed your cutting horse. Some horses may not require any grain at all, whereas others need various portions in order to gain weight, raise the energy level, or put a bloom in their coats.

I grain my cutting horses every day, but the amount is quite small (a double handful) unless I feel their energy is ebbing, or if the temperature has dropped below zero. Because they are in good condition and my hay is high quality, the grain is more of a treat for them, and a good way to get them to eat supplements. Also, I find graining to be one more excuse to enter each horse's stall daily and check on his well-being.

Salt

Salt should be available to your horse at all times because it helps regulate the fluid balance in his body. Salt can be fed in loose form or, more easily, in a solid block. If your soil is deficient in iodine, feed iodized salt to ensure proper thyroid function. Otherwise plain or trace-mineralized salt is best.

Supplements

Commercially made vitamin supplements, when used in moderation, will ensure your horse's health. But these supplements vary greatly in potency, and it's wise to check first with your vet or county agent to determine which balance will best match your area and your horse's requirements.

Veterinary Care

The best thing you can do for your horse is to use a good veterinarian. He will help you plan a worming and vaccination program to fit your horse's particular needs, advise you about feeding and supplements, and take care of dental and medical problems. Establish a good relationship with your vet: He is worth every penny.

I asked a vet friend of mine what he felt was the ideal "barn call." He said his best customers were those who were ready for him when he arrived, whose horses were broke and relatively manageable, who knew basic equine first aid, and who allowed him to do his work and helped out only when asked.

Teeth

The condition of a horse's teeth is of utmost importance. They reflect his overall fitness as well as the way he reacts to a bit. Even yearlings should have their teeth checked periodically because the premolars, or wolf teeth, may need to be removed. Also sharp or jagged edges can develop, even on the teeth of youngsters. These edges need to be rasped down once or twice a year.

Be aware that dental problems may exist if, for instance, your horse has a tendency to throw his head or to fight the bit, or if you notice that he dribbles food while eating.

Farrier

Using a quality farrier is also something not to be overlooked. This person should be familiar with how a cutting horse moves and handles himself in order to shoe your horse properly. Some horses need more support than others, some need more support in the hind end, and some may have special problems that a farrier can help to remedy. There are several different types of shoes and methods of shoeing available nowadays, and there are differing opinions to go along with each. Your best bet is to ask another cutter to recommend a good farrier.

Grooming

Your horse's coat will blossom with daily grooming. Go over the trunk of his body with a rubber curry to loosen dirt, then brush him from head to toe. If you have a vacuum designed for horses, use it as a follow-up. Although not a necessity, the vacuum is a wonderful invention because it takes out the finest dust from any coat and stimulates natural oil production.

Manes and tails require extra care. Most riders avoid daily brushing of these areas other than to remove tangles or sawdust. Aside from the forelock (which should be short enough to allow a horse to easily see a cow) you can encourage full growth of the mane and tail by avoiding harsh combs and by using a good hair softener and conditioner after every washing. Save more thorough grooming for a show. To preserve or increase the fullness in your horse's tail, tie up the longer strands in ten or fifteen small, loose knots. When they come undone, just tie them up again. Or tie his tail in one big knot each time you train, and fasten it with a rubber band. Another solution, although it can be annoying to a horse, is to keep his tail braided.

4

TACK AND
TRAINING AIDS:
THE TOOLS OF
THE TRADE

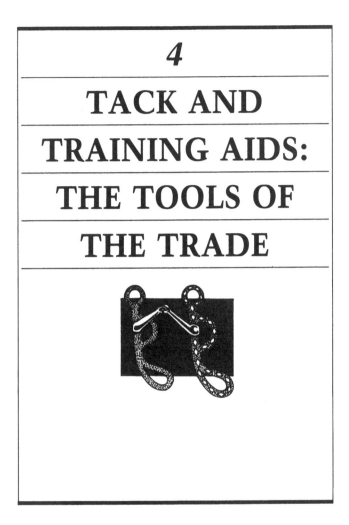

A cutting horse requires slightly different equipment from other western horses because of the speed and the quick directional changes he makes to stay even with a cow. Tack and a few of the more widely used training aids are discussed here to indicate what can be used in training as well as what is popular for showing.

Saddle

First designed in Texas by Buster Welch and Windy Ryan, a cutting saddle is specially made to help the rider stay balanced and above a horse's center of gravity during the very dramatic movements that occur in cutting. The saddle serves as a shock absorber, yet it is very light and made to sit down close to a horse's back so that you can *feel* every movement underneath you.

The seat is larger than that of other western saddles, to allow you to move around a little without being "locked" into one position. The saddle horn is higher so that you can comfortably push against it for maximum leverage to maintain balance. The fenders are fairly narrow so that you can easily change your leg position when helping a horse or staying out of his way.

There are almost as many saddlemakers as there are saddles, and choosing one from such a large market can be confusing. Your individual body frame will be the main consideration, and a good trainer or a tack store specializing in cutting saddles will be the best sources to help find one that suits you. Bigger competitions around the country always have displays and representatives from major tack supply stores. These salesmen know the cutting business well. You can also find information in such horse publications as *The Cuttin' Hoss Chatter* and *The Quarter Horse News*, which are full of advertisements for saddles and tack.

When looking at a cutting saddle, consider the following:

- Every saddle is built around a foundation called a "tree." Find a saddlemaker who has a good reputation with cutting horse people for manufacturing sturdy trees.
- The seat should be fairly flat and with a cantle that slopes so that you don't hit the rear. It should feel comfortable, giving you enough room to slide around during hard stops and turns. Saddles come with rough seats and slick seats; if you want to break in your purchase quickly and avoid a few sores, get a slick one.
- The size of seat depends upon your body frame. Most cutters, male or female, ride with a 16 or 16½ inch seat, but you'll need a bigger one if you have a large frame.
- Some horns are built higher or with more of a slant than others. Your torso and arm length will be the determining factors in comfort and preference. If you are uncertain, ask a pro or a sales rep for some guidance.

When you see a saddle you like, check to make sure that it fits your horse properly with only a light pad underneath. Because some riders have the tendency to place a saddle too far forward over a horse's withers, be sure to position the saddle so it sits in the *middle* of his back. Then, if possible, work him on some cows while you test it. When your horse is warm, take off the saddle and look at the wet area underneath. If there are dry places or areas with evidence of rubbing or irritation, the saddle is not fitting his back correctly. Using a thicker saddle pad will help to remedy these problems, but the basic fit should be close and even.

Stirrups

A good stirrup for cutting should fit your foot, feel comfortable, and not inhibit the movement of your boot or spur. Usually made of aluminum or iron, it is shaped either in an oxbow or with a flat bottom. The popular depth of the covered rawhide platform ranges from 1 to 2 inches, although there are wider ones available.

When looking for a stirrup, try different styles before you buy. Find one that allows you a good base without hurting the sides of your foot. If you'll be doing a lot of training, then a flat bottom may be more comfortable. Mike Haack uses this type when he's training horses because he feels it is easier to kick free should a colt fall.

> I like the feel of a 1½ inch oxbow because it gives me a good platform, and I know that my foot will stay deep in the stirrup under the arch of my foot. My boot is a ladies size 8, but many men use the same size and style. Again, stirrups are a matter of personal preference.

Cinch or Girth

A cutting horse learns to move not only in response to a cow, but to the rider's leg and spur pressing against different areas of his sides. A cinch is positioned correctly when the saddle sits in the middle of the horse instead of too far forward. There should be room enough to use your spur just in front of that cinch as well as behind it.

There are two types of cinches, fleece-lined and webbed. Opinions differ as to which is better. Padded cinches, if kept clean, do an excellent job of preventing sores and are often used on younger horses. Webbed cinches are not as bulky or wide, making it easier to place your leg and spur in a certain area to achieve the desired response.

Whichever cinch you decide to use, make sure your horse's belly is toughened up first. To do this, some pros will loosely saddle their young colts two or three hours each day before they are ridden. After working the colts, the pros check them for any signs of soreness, and use another type of cinch if soreness is found.

Back Cinch

Although some riders don't use a back cinch when they are training, almost all have one on their favorite competition saddle (out of deference to tradition, if nothing else). A back cinch is designed to hold the back of a saddle down during hard stops and turns, but some pros feel that it can confuse a horse because it tends to hit against the same area as a leg or spur. You'll see a variety of fits (and you'll hear a variety of opinions). Some cinches are snugged up against the horse's belly with only room for a hand to slide underneath, and others are adjusted so loosely that a horse could catch his foot in it.

Saddle Pads

Most cutters use one or two thick blankets under a saddle when training at home to protect a horse's back and withers, and also to let his back "breathe." These blankets are made of felt or fleece, and often are covered on one side with woven fabric for a nicer look. Because of sweat and dirt buildup, whatever material is used should be easy to wash.

For competition, a favorite Navajo blanket or woven saddle pad looks quite nice on a horse's back. It can be used by itself, allowing the rider to be as close as possible to the horse, or it can be placed on top of another pad.

Headstalls

A bridle can be plain or fancy, complete with silver conchas or horsehair woven into the sides. Whether for training at home or showing in competition, a good quality plain leather headstall with a throatlatch is popular. It assures that a bit will hang squarely in the horse's mouth. Also popular are

Trainer Dave Hammond keeps his tack room in top shape. The bits and bosals are arranged according to type, with each set of reins draped around the wooden peg. Saddles are kept on racks, and every blanket sits on top to keep the dust from accumulating. The blankets are turned over to allow for easy drying after being used on a horse.

split-ear and half sliding-ear headstalls with a little bit of silver. These headstalls should not inhibit the movement of a horse's ear in any way, and they need to be adjusted to allow the bit to hang evenly in his mouth.

Bits

Though little has been written about the subject, finding the right bit for your horse is one of the most important aspects of training. A bit needs to fit the size and shape of a horse's mouth and allow for variations in his teeth and his bite. It should suit his needs and yours too, for, aside from your legs, a bit is the way you communicate with your horse.

Numerous bits are on the market today, and finding the correct one for your horse takes guidance or a great deal of experience and "feel." Every trainer seems to have his own arsenal that includes old favorites as well as some newer ones he's experimenting with. He wants, as does any good horseman, to find ways to keep each horse's mouth light and responsive throughout training. If a horse feels a little numb, throws his head, or fights a particular bit, then the rider will analyze the reason and try another bit.

Mouthpieces are made of stainless steel, iron, or copper. Iron bits rust quickly, and many people feel that rust helps a horse salivate and keeps his mouth "sweet" or soft. Iron-core mouthpieces covered with copper, and stainless steel ones with strips of copper accomplish much the same thing; they are equally popular because horses seem to like the taste of both.

Cheeks and shanks of bits are made of aluminum, stainless steel, or blued steel. The outside can be plain or inlaid with silver or nickel designs.

Following are descriptions of some of the more common bits, hacka-mores, and training devices used on cutting horses. Many are not allowed to be used during competition because they are considered aids or gimmicks that give the rider undue control over his horse (it's wise to stay current with the NCHA rules about equipment if you wish to compete in an approved or sponsored cutting event).

Snaffles

Smooth-mouth or ring snaffle. This is designed for lateral pull, and is used primarily in starting young horses. Some snaffles are mild, having a thicker mouthpiece that tapers in toward the center, while some are thin and more severe. Since there are many versions of a snaffle bit and since weight and feel can vary so much, it's best to get a professional to help you find a good one to fit your horse.

Whichever snaffle you choose, be sure that it is wide enough not to pinch your horse's mouth. Adjust the headstall so that the bit sits fairly low (one wrinkle on either side of his mouth). This encourages your horse to "carry" it in his mouth. A proper fit also helps prevent unnecessary sores from developing.

Twisted-wire snaffle. Good for a horse with a mouth that is dull or unre-sponsive to a regular snaffle. However, it may be too severe for a youngster, especially when used for more than a few days at a time.

Argentine snaffle. Designed to produce more lateral pull on a fairly well-broke horse. Good for a stiff horse, and also good to school with because of increased leverage when you pull back. It has a loose-jawed shank, and is often used as a bridge when changing from a snaffle to a curb bit because it is milder than the curb.

Curb Bits

Grazing bit. An all-purpose bit used after basic training has been done, it consists of a curved iron or steel mouthpiece set between two sidepieces. The mouthpiece can have a high, medium, or low port, depending upon the feel you want to get. The sidepieces, or shanks, are made of aluminum, stainless steel, or blued steel, and come in different lengths depending upon desired leverage and feel.

Probably the more popular grazing bit for a younger horse, or for a "finished" older horse with a soft mouth, it has a low port and aluminum shanks. It is light yet versatile, depending on how tight you make the curb chain. An older horse may need a higher port in his mouth to make him respect the bit.

Some people feel a curb bit should fit low in a cutting horse's mouth so that it helps him maintain his natural head position and encourages him to reach lower to hold it.

C Bit. A sweet iron, low port bit with short, stainless steel cheeks or shanks, often used on a colt before putting him into a grazing bit.

Bosal or Hackamore

Many trainers start a colt in a rope noseband hackamore instead of a bit, especially if there are any problems with his teeth or the shape of his mouth. Bosals are also used at different times during training to let a horse rest from constantly having a bit in his mouth.

Bosals come in a variety of sizes and weights. Medium-size bosals covered with cloth or latigo leather are easier on a horse's nose; they are softer and don't need to be shaped to the horse's jaw and nose like the stiffer ones made with rawhide. Larger bosals can often be more severe if they are stiff and made to fit fairly snugly against a horse's jaw; they are used to lighten up a heavy-headed horse. Bosals that are made with a bicycle chain over the nose area are hard on a horse's nose, but easier on his chin.

> A bosal can easily be misused. A rider's hard-handedness and bad temper can tear up a horse's cheek and chin.

A steel-band hackamore is essentially of the same design, but with more "bite" to it. It is good to use occasionally on a colt that pulls on the rope hackamore. He'll feel it against his nose and will quickly learn to soften up again.

Metal Noseband with Shanks

Good on a horse that has trouble responding to the rider when asked to stop. The shanks provide extra leverage to an iron bosal.

Sidepull

Sidepulls help lateral movement by taking a horse's nose to one side without hurting his mouth at all. A rope sidepull is often used when starting a colt or even after he is accustomed to a snaffle. A rawhide one is for a horse that doesn't have a very sensitive nose. Steel nosebands or ones made of a piece of bicycle chain are used occasionally during training, when a rider wants to keep away from a horse's mouth. Using them takes skill, for they have a lot of bite.

Quick Stop

This device has a rawhide noseband attached in back to a metal piece that presses against a horse's jaw when pulled back. It can be very severe on a horse; its only purpose is to make him stop quickly.

Additional Tack

Chin Strap

Chin straps are used to loosely connect the rings of a snaffle bit or to create "feel" and more leverage on other types of bits. They are made of plain leather (for use on a lighter-mouthed or sensitive horse), chain with nylon, or chain with leather.

Though a chin strap should be very loose when on a snaffle bit, it needs to be adjusted properly on other bits. If too loose, nothing is accomplished, while one that is too tight can rub and irritate a horse's chin, eventually causing him to become insensitive to it. With a correct fit, you should be able to insert two fingers between the strap and the horse's chin groove.

Running Martingale

This device is fairly popular when used with a sidepull, snaffle, or light curb bit because it encourages a horse to keep his head low and his nose in position during training. It is not, however, a substitute for a good pair of hands. When using a martingale, be careful not to adjust it too tightly, for it will force a horse's nose downward when you pull on the reins, and thus become more of a punishment than a training aid. Adjust the length so that the rings reach the top of your horse's shoulder at the level where you usually hold your hands.

Reins

Reins made of harness leather are popular because they hang well, have some weight to them, and become quite pliable after being used and conditioned with a good leather cleaner. Proper thickness depends on how they feel in an individual's hands, but most cutters prefer them to be ⅝ or ½ inches wide. A popular length is about 7 feet.

Breast Collar

A breast collar prevents a saddle from slipping back. Many riders like to use a simple breast collar when riding in competition, if only for decoration.

Splint Boots

Whenever you're schooling a horse or working him on a cow, the condition of his legs is of prime importance. Well-padded splint boots help to protect him from hurting his splint bones, cannon bones, and ligaments as he makes quick turns and stops. They are cheap insurance. The boots should fit securely and should be made with a fairly soft, washable material so they won't irritate a horse's legs. Keeping them clean will help prevent ringbone or "scratches."

Most cutters use splint boots on the front legs of every horse they ride. However, if the horse sits down hard on his hocks or has a tendency to step on his back legs, it's a good idea to protect the back legs with boots too.

Skid Boots

A horse that naturally stops "deep" in the ground (brings his hind legs under him and skids to a halt) can burn his fetlocks. And once he hurts himself, he's less likely to try to stop as hard. Skid boots on the back feet can prevent this from happening.

The Rider's Tools

Spurs

Spurs are an *aid* to the rider's leg, not a weapon. As with any bit, you need to develop a feel for a spur before you can use it properly, and you need to become aware of each horse's level of sensitivity to it. The angle and shank length of a spur will depend upon how long your legs are. Normal shank length is 1½ inches. The type of rowel you choose should balance your aggressiveness as a rider. A popular flat, cloverleaf rowel allows you to "press" it into a horse's sides without scaring him. A sharper rowel requires much more care when being used.

Competition Apparel

Cutting horse riders are fairly conservative when it comes to dress, and it's in your best interest to fit in with the crowd to some degree when entering competition. The difference between winning and losing is often as small as half a point, so you'll want to do everything in your power to look professional and self-assured when walking into that arena. Bright red boots, white chaps, and a purple hat will not paint the picture of someone who's there to cut cattle and win with a score of 76. It's tough enough to impress a judge and earn points without waving a red flag at him, as if saying "I'm new to this, and you'll have an easy job spotting the errors of a novice." So take a good look at what the successful riders are wearing, whether at club cuttings or at big shows, and adapt to their ways.

Chaps

Chaps are optional attire, but almost every cutter wears them in competition. Chaps are also worn during winter training when it's cold, or when accustoming a two-year-old to the sight and feel of them next to his sides. A good way to choose a pair is to look at the popular styles at a big show and then talk to some of the store representatives. They can guide you toward finding a nicely fitted pair or will measure you for custom ones. Also, most every western supply store carries both standardized and custom chaps.

Popular today are either roughout batwing (with or without fringe) chaps or shotgun chaps with fringe. Little extras such as trim, tooling, stamped patterns, and silver can be added according to your taste. As for color, something in tan tones is customary.

Boots

Whatever your requirements and taste, nice boots can be found to suit you. Most cutters have a durable pair of work boots for everyday use, and a pair of dress boots for evening wear. Some cutters also have a good looking pair just for showing in competition. How they are made and what they are made of is entirely a matter of individual preference and comfort.

Jeans

Wrangler is the official jeans company of the NCHA, supporting many cutting events in the country. Wearing their label is a nice way to thank them. But Levi's jeans are popular too. Both of these companies have had the corner on the western market for quite a long time, although there is always room for something new. Blue is the most common color, yet black, tan, or gray jeans are often seen.

Shirts

Shirts must conform to the rules of the NCHA if you are appearing in an approved show (these rules are in the NCHA *Rule Book* and should be checked each year for changes). At present, shirts must be long-sleeved with collars and buttons or snaps. Because shirts can be of any color or design, this is where you can add some individuality to your "look" in the arena.

> Men are still fairly conservative in the color choice and design of their shirts, but women have loosened up a bit. Depending on the day or my mood, I'll wear anything from white to bright pink or turquoise, with stripes and designs. It's nice to have a variety when I'm on the road, because shirts are the one item that helps me feel like an individual.

Hats

Western hats are a requirement in an NCHA-approved show arena. Shapes, brims, and creases vary slightly, but it's pretty easy to spot those that don't fit the norm. Stetson and Resistol both sponsor many cutting events and, again, it's nice to show them your support. Popular colors for winter hats are gray, beige, or plain black. Summer hats are made of natural-colored straw. Riders often individualize their cowboy hats by putting a narrow horsehair or colored band around the brim. Anything overly noticeable is, again, a way of standing out too much from other competitors.

Choosing the right tack and clothing for training or competition may seem overwhelming if you are new to the sport of cutting. But with a little experience and some good advice, you'll find items to suit you and your horse. Get started off right, and go for the basics. You can branch out and get more technical later on.

5

BASIC RIDER

POSITION

A horse reflects the
way you ride
–LINDY BURCH

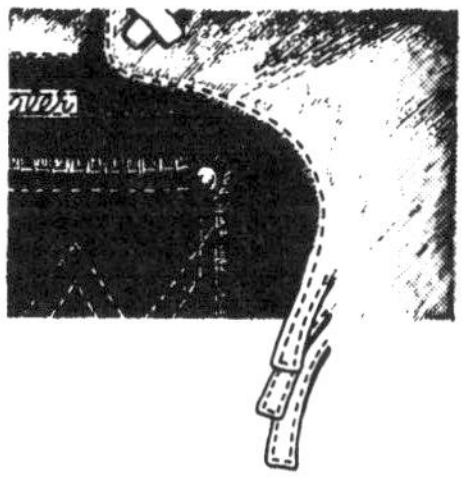

Newcomers to cutting have little understanding of why a certain experienced rider might prefer a different angle for his saddle horn, or a specially made rowel on his spur, or why he might have his stirrups shaped differently from someone else's. They don't realize the importance of a rider's leg action, correct rein use, and balance in the saddle. With a little bit of experience these factors will begin to take on importance, and what appeared to be fairly simple will seem a lot more complex. Everything must fit together just right to make cutting look easy.

Trainer Julie Roddy demonstrates the balanced position a cutter maintains while working a cow. She sits upright and faces the cow. Her right hand is pushing against the saddle horn while her left is holding the reins and touching her horse's neck. Her legs are loose and out of the horse's way during his turn.

The way you sit a saddle, handle the reins, and use your legs and spurs are critical to a horse's performance, because he responds not only to what a cow does but to what *you* do as a rider. Even if an experienced trainer rides your colt most of the time, the horse may react differently when you climb aboard. Try to learn all you can about the mechanics of your own body position *before* you try to work your cutting horse on a cow. Though they may seem basic, these skills are essential if you are to train and stay in sync with a cutting horse's athletic and explosive movements. As well-known pro Chubby Turner says, "You've got to be in step if you want to dance with your partner."

This book assumes that you already know how to ride, that your horse is at least "green-broke" (meaning that he has learned to respond to basic signals and will give in to rein and leg pressure), and that he has been "legged-up" (or conditioned) in the hills and on the flat for a month or two. This chapter expands upon those basics and relates them to the art of cutting. Keep an open mind while trying out the ideas set forth here, for each horse and each rider is going to be somewhat different, and each situation will call for slight adjustments.

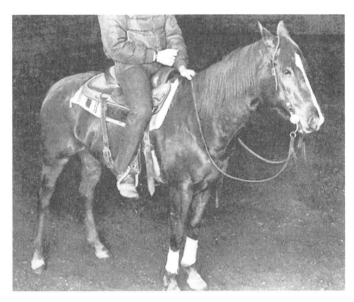

The way to sit a saddle is to be relaxed and comfortable so that you can feel the horse underneath you. Torso facing straight ahead; arms relaxed and low; one hand on the saddle horn and the other resting on the horse's neck; reins loose and even; seat fully relaxed as if sitting in a chair; legs at a comfortable angle; feet pushed deep into the stirrups. In this position, you are best able to help your horse.

Body Position

Any rider who attends a good cutting clinic is bound to hear a phrase that has found its way from physics into cow cutting philosophy: *For every action there is a reaction.* Let's look at body position and basic horse-handling with that idea in mind.

The key to riding a horse well is *balance*, and balance is the result of good body position in the saddle. It's important to find and maintain a position that is comfortable and natural so that your weight remains evenly distributed over a horse's center of gravity, no matter how dramatic a move he may make when reacting to a cow. With this balance you can easily use your legs to help him speed up or finish his turns without impeding his natural action in any way.

Head and Torso

Let's look first at your upper body and how it relates to the way you ride. Your torso, like your seat, should be considered as part of your horse. As long as it remains balanced, quiet, and facing straight ahead, you will not adversely affect a horse's movements. However, any stiffness, leaning, or twisting will upset that balance and cause the negative reactions listed on the following page.

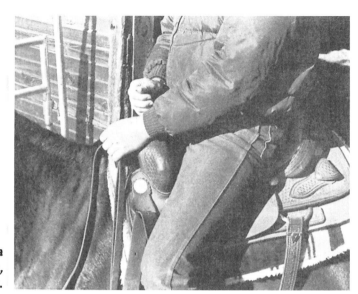

The correct way to sit a saddle, hold the reins, and hold the saddle horn.

- By *trying* to sit up too straight, you'll become stiff. Three related responses will occur: You'll flop around as your horse changes speed and direction; this upper body movement will cause your legs to grip the horse's sides; and your horse will feel the pressure on his sides and think you want him to go forward just when you might want him to stop.
- Leaning back or sideways will also cause you to be stiff and unbalanced, with the same results. If you lean when your horse is in the process of stopping and turning with a cow, you'll actually be telling him to make rounded turns and to "leak" (come out toward the cow) instead of staying back.
- Twisting your torso one way or the other will affect the way your legs rest against a horse's sides, again causing him to misinterpret what you want him to do.

To understand the connection between upper and lower body, sit down in the saddle and experiment. Lean back. Are your legs compensating by stiffening up? Are you putting extra weight on the stirrups? Leaning back, even for a moment, puts your legs out of good working position. Each leg must be relaxed and free in order to help a horse speed up or finish his turns.

Now, twist to the left or right. Can you feel knee and leg pressure against your horse's sides? What happens when you lean to one side—where is that leg pressure? Are you standing (and, thus, immobile) in one of the stirrups? Did your horse step over or otherwise shift his weight to compensate?

What about your head? You can look in any direction as long as your shoulders and torso remain facing straight ahead. In fact, when you are working a cow, both eyes should be focused on that cow at all times, *never* on your horse.

> Often at cuttings I'll notice a rider who is so intent on watching the cow that his whole body turns to face it, instead of just his head. This inevitably causes a chain reaction, with the end result being the loss of working position on that cow.

Hands and Arms

You are centered in the saddle, relaxed and in a good position. Now let's look at your hands and arms.

Unless you are using both hands on the reins during training, one will almost always be on the saddle horn. The horn is designed to help you nestle down in the saddle so that you'll remain centered and balanced when a horse stops and turns with a cow. By pushing against it, you can prevent your upper body from falling forward onto the horse's front end and causing him to compensate for the extra weight.

Basically (although there are slight variations), the horn is held much like a gearshift: thumb somewhere on the top, fingers wrapped loosely around it, and the heel of the hand pushing against it. Bend your arm as if you are about to shake hands with someone, then lock your elbow next to your hip.

> An easy way to get the feel of using the saddle horn is to push against it whenever you are loping a horse, either during a warm-up or when you're out riding in the hills.

Holding and using the reins are things every rider seems to take for granted, but it's an art. Your reins connect you to a horse's mouth. They are used to show direction, check forward movement, and to stop or back up. They can be held in either hand or both, depending on the bit you're using and whether you are training or showing. They should remain even at all times unless you *purposely* intend to pull your horse's nose to one side.

Holding the reins when using a snaffle bit. The rider's hands are low and wide apart, and his wrists are straight so that he can pull back with his arms and shoulders. The thumbs and elbows are low, and the bit contact is through his fingers, which act as cushions to the strength of the arm movement. This way, the rider can keep a horse's head in line with his body.

Learning how to use reins requires skill and timing. Although trainers vary in the degree to which they rely on reins, most will avoid overuse. A horse that worries about his mouth and what the reins are telling him will react to his rider all the time instead of to the cow. One of the golden rules of training is to let the *cow* teach the horse how to respond.

The amount of slack to allow in the reins depends on what you are trying to accomplish. For schooling, adjust the reins so that they are loose enough only to allow your horse's head some freedom of movement. This way, you can correct him quickly without first having to pull up lots of slack. In competition, the reins are held much more loosely so that it's obvious to a judge that you are not controlling your horse's head or mouth. However, reins shouldn't be held so loose that they look sloppy or get in the way of the horse.

- *Using the reins with a snaffle bit.* Most often, you'll hold a rein in each hand when using a snaffle to easily show a colt direction and balance. Hold your arms at a fairly low and relaxed angle so that you don't elevate the colt's head when pulling back. Keep your hands apart

Tipping a colt's nose to the right when using a snaffle bit. Pull the rein back toward your hip just enough to tip the colt's nose in the direction you want him to go. The rider's right leg is relaxed and out of the horse's way, and the left leg presses him in the belly to further encourage him to turn.

Tipping a colt's nose to the left with a snaffle bit to begin a turn. The left hand is supporting his nose and giving him direction. The right hand supports the right side of the bit, the neck, and the shoulder in order to prevent his rear end from coming out in the turn.

so that they are almost in line with your knees. This way, your colt will be encouraged to stay lower in front where he can better see and concentrate on a cow. He'll also be able to see your hands when you help him turn to the left or right.

Trainer Dan Manning demonstrates the use of reins to correct his horse when working in an Argentine snaffle. He uses his other hand to take up the slack when working on a loose rein.

- Holding the reins too tight will interfere with a horse's concentration; he'll feel the bit in his mouth and worry about the rider instead of thinking about the cow.
- Holding the reins too loose can also cause problems: Whenever you needed to stop or hold his forward motion, you would have to pull those reins clear up to your *chin* to take up the slack. This would elevate the horse's head and take his attention away from the cow.

Reins can also be held in just one hand when a colt is moving properly in a snaffle, but make certain that the reins are kept even so that you don't inadvertently "bump" the bit on one side. Do not attempt to neck-rein with a snaffle bit, because when the rein drags across a horse's neck, it will actually pull his head in the wrong direction.

- *Using the reins with a curb bit.* A rider holds the reins *evenly* in one hand when using a curb bit, with his arm low and his hand close to the horse's neck just in front of the saddle horn. When you want to check your horse's forward movement, stop it altogether, or back him up, pull the reins slightly toward your hip or belt buckle. Pull directly so as not to elevate his head. The degree to which you pull depends on the horse and what you want him to do. If he's responsive to you (as he should be), he'll only need to feel a *suggestion* of the reins being lifted before he slows down, stops, or backs. Be sure that your reins are even when pulling back on them. If your horse tips his head to one side, use your free hand on the rein to even him up.

It's useful to become accustomed to holding the reins in either hand so that during training you can easily switch, in order to help your horse maintain a certain body or head position. To develop this flexibility, cross your reins over so they lie on each side of his neck. Pick them up in the middle with one hand and then switch to the other hand, making sure the reins remain even.

Seat

The seat of a cutting saddle is fairly flat so that the rider can sit in the *middle* and have ample room to slide around during hard stops and turns. Sit it like a saddle-bronc rider: in the middle of the saddle without coming in contact with the back (the cantle). Tilt your pelvis so that you sink down and sit on your blue-jeans pockets. Now you're centered and in a position to melt into the seat when the going gets tough. You've become a part of your horse, and you can exhibit readiness and confidence.

> If you sit against the back of a saddle on a cutting horse, your body can easily be thrown forward and out of position anytime there is dramatic movement. Sit, instead, so that you can run your hand between your bottom and the cantle.

Leg Position and Use

A cutting horse's speed and direction often will need to be corrected by the rider to maintain proper position on a cow. This is done when one or both of your legs come into contact with certain areas of his sides. In order to make the best use of your legs for control, first make sure that your stirrups are properly adjusted, and that you understand the mechanics of leg action and placement.

Stirrup Length

To find the correct stirrup length, sit comfortably in the middle of the saddle and push your boots deep into each stirrup almost to where your heels hit the metal. If your legs rest in a reasonable and relaxed bend, the stirrup length is correct. You have good leg position when you can draw an imaginary straight line from your shoulder to hip to the back of your heel. Experiment with several lengths to feel the differences, keeping in mind that shorter stirrups restrict lower leg movement, while longer stirrups invite a rider to brace his legs against them instead of remaining relaxed.

Leg and Foot Position

When your feet are in the stirrups, your lower legs should rest alongside the cinch, forming a line perpendicular to it. Don't put much weight on the stirrups, and point your toes slightly outward. Your knees shouldn't be touching the saddle fenders. It's almost as if you were riding with no stirrups at all. Although this position may not win any prizes in western equitation, you *will* be able to ride a cutting horse. By sitting deeper and more relaxed in the saddle, you can stay loose in your knees and avoid gripping. You also can use your legs and spurs easily.

> I still have to concentrate on foot position every time I ride; it's not quite automatic when things get going fast. Sometimes I'll rock forward in the saddle and accidently spur my horse, just because my toes are pointed down instead of out. And if I'm tense and my toes aren't pointed outward, the inevitable happens: I grip with my knees and cause both legs to become rigid and useless, which my horse interprets as *go* instead of *whoa*. This doesn't happen to every rider, however. Trainer Bill Freeman rides with his feet pointed straight ahead and legs wrapped around his horse's belly. But Bill's reaction time is a lot quicker than mine, and he can make slight adjustments without confusing his horse.

Spurs

Spurs are used to help a horse learn to react more quickly to leg pressure. As mentioned earlier, they are intended to be an *aid* to the rider's leg, never a weapon. Learning when and how to use a spur takes experience and a lot of

Use your spur near the back cinch to move a horse's hind end.

"feel," for spurs can cause major problems when applied at the wrong time and for the wrong reasons.

You can't use your spur if it's not pointing toward your horse. This fact emphasizes the importance of leg position. With your feet pushed deep in the stirrups, point your toes out in an exaggerated way and slowly swing each leg back and forth. At some point in the arc of that movement, your spur can make contact with the horse and cause him to react. And because he will move away from pressure, you can make him move his shoulder, or his belly, or his hip simply by pressing in slightly different areas: just in front of the cinch, just behind, or back a little farther in the flank, respectively.

> Here's an example of the importance of spur placement: Once I tried to back a young colt in a straight line without much success. The backing part was fine, but he kept moving his hip to the left. I attempted to correct him by pressing my left spur into his belly next to the cinch, but it wasn't until I moved my heel back further on the flank that he responded and straightened out his line.

There are several ways to get your horse's attention with a spur if he doesn't react to your calf. Normally, if pushed, or "pressed," with a spur, he'll move away from that pressure. *Press* does not mean *tickle*, nor does it mean

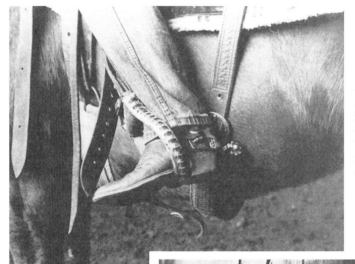

Use your spur just be-hind the cinch to arc the horse's rib cage away from the spur pressure. This is the most common place to use a spur.

Use your spur just to the front of the cinch to move the front end.

harpoon. To press means to push a spur against an area and keep it there only long enough to get the required response. If your horse doesn't move away, simply press harder. And if this doesn't get a reaction, run the rowel quickly up and down his side. Cutters call this rowel use "zinging." It makes a noise, *and* an impression, and it's almost guaranteed that the next time you need to press your spur into him, he'll be more willing to listen.

Gina MacDonald demonstrates "zinging" a spur. Your legs must be positioned as if you were sitting on a barrel with your toes turned out. Lift your leg while simultaneously lifting your heel and rolling the rowel up and down the horse's belly.

Be aware that a stallion will often respond to a spur differently than a mare or gelding. His instinct is to move *in toward* pressure instead of *away* from it.

Using a spur more than is needed will cause any horse to be resentful and iron-sided. *A horse learns by being rewarded, not punished.* If you need to reinforce what you've asked of him with your leg, press your spur into him and then leave him alone. Reward means a release from pressure.

6

HANDLING YOUR HORSE: THE FUNDAMENTALS

A young horse should be green-broke, fairly strong, and physically fit before he's brought into a training program for cutting. He should have been legged-up for three or four months in the hills or on open land to build muscle and to learn to accept saddle and rider with confidence. This "breaking" process usually begins when a colt is between twenty and twenty-four months old, although much depends on the degree of his development and his owner's plans for competition. From then through the two, three, or four years that it takes to build the skills required of a cutting horse, he will participate in a consistent training program. That means many hours of repetition and much exposure to cattle.

Movement, balance, and communication between horse and rider are building blocks in the development of a good cutting horse. Before working full time on cattle, a colt should know how to travel in a straight line, to stop and back up straight, to move off the rider's leg, and to walk in small circles with an even bend in his body.

Some trainers feel that it is also important for a colt to turn around on his hocks, or pivot. This move, although it has no relation to cutting a cow, will help a colt learn to use his body and get his legs well underneath himself.

These basics often are overlooked, either because a rider has too many horses to train or because he doesn't think it necessary to spend much time with "dry work" (without using cattle). But they're important if you expect a horse to understand what you want. Giving your horse a solid foundation should not be confused with *excessive* dry work, however; you are not training a reined cow horse that takes most of his cues from the rider. You're training a horse to learn to react to a cow.

I learned something about basics after having bought a six-year-old mare that had been ridden in the aged events. She had no problem watching and reacting to a cow, but she wouldn't listen to me when I tried to shorten up her stops and asked her to finish each turn completely. When I asked trainer Bobby Nelson for some help, he rode her for only a minute or two before suggesting that first I get her broke. It was an accurate assessment.

Moving Forward
in a Straight Line

Your horse should know how to walk, trot, and lope in a straight line and do so in a relaxed and confident manner. When done correctly, he will have the basics of collection, control, and balance.

> Moving in a straight line isn't as easy as it sounds. When I'm riding a two-year-old at a walk, for example, it sometimes feels as though his front end and back end aren't quite aligned. I then need to concentrate on using my legs, making slight adjustments until he moves in a straight line on his own.

To ask your horse to move forward at a walk, run your rein hand slightly up his neck and squeeze with the calves of your legs. If he needs any extra prodding to move, lightly press both spurs into his belly just behind the cinch. Once started, remember to use your legs, not your reins, to keep his body moving in a straight line, so that his head and neck remain in a low and relaxed position. Hold the reins low and just loose enough not to "bump" the bit in his mouth.

Then move him into an easy trot, again making sure you correct his line of movement with your legs if and when a correction is needed. During trotting is a good time to check your own position in the saddle. Keep your upper body quiet, and hold the reins low and even. Try to relax your pelvis and move in sync with your horse. If you stiffen up and begin to grip his sides with your legs, he will think you are asking him to go faster.

To extend the trot, use your legs to squeeze your horse forward. If the faster pace is too difficult to sit to without bouncing around, you can stand up in the stirrups and hold on to the saddle horn. Or you can "post" up and down, as if you were riding on an English saddle.

Loping in a straight line can be more difficult for a rider only because everything happens faster. Pick an imaginary line to follow, and concentrate solely on using your legs (hands too, if needed) to help your colt move naturally and straight along that line.

> Something that helped me learn how to relax in the middle of the saddle was to push against the saddle horn with the palm of my hand whenever I loped a horse. I could then feel every move.

Stopping

A good straight stop is the foundation for every turn or forward motion that a cutting horse will need in order to match, counter, and control a cow's

Stopping a colt when using a snaffle bit. Hands are low and wide apart, wrists serve as a cushion for each arm as the reins are pulled back toward the hip.

Stopping a more experienced colt or horse when using an Argentine snaffle or a curb bit. One hand pulls the reins back toward the rider's hip, while the other pushes against the saddle horn.

movements. The minute you sink down deep in the saddle and pick up slightly on the reins, your horse should respond by sitting down squarely on his haunches. It should feel almost as if he has folded into himself to keep from hitting a brick wall. He will be straight, correct, balanced, and unafraid as long as your legs are out of his sides and you are not elevating his front end or jerking on his nose or mouth. That powerhouse of a hind end will be coiled underneath him, so he'll be ready to move off in any direction.

Don't expect a young colt to have a perfect stop. If he has been trained to stop properly, he'll react quickly when you pick up on the reins and sit down deeper in the saddle. But his stop won't be crisp, and it may not be as straight as you would like. Asking him to "sit down in the ground" when he's still in this early two-year-old stage can easily cause damage to his legs, not to mention his mind. So don't overdo the practice, and don't be in a hurry for him to make perfect stops. A youngster can't take the pressure you might put on a more mature horse. Better stops will develop naturally as your colt learns to move with a cow.

The preparatory command to ask a horse to stop is *sitting down deep in the saddle*. This does not mean leaning back with your upper body, but, instead, hunkering down like a bull rider and sitting on your blue jeans hip pockets. Let your legs relax so that they stay away from the horse's sides. Not only is this a signal that he will learn to associate with stopping, but you are also preparing yourself to remain as well balanced and quiet as possible during that stop.

Almost simultaneously, pull the reins evenly and firmly back toward your hip. The moment your horse stops, give him slack. That's his reward.

The angle you use when pulling back on the reins is quite important. A *reining horse* (or working cow horse) is elevated in front when he slides to a stop, but a *cutting horse* should be relaxed and low so that he's almost eye-to-eye with the cow he is working. If you elevate his front end by pulling the reins back toward your chest or chin, he cannot stay connected with the cow. He's going to be thinking about *you* instead of his job. This is also true when you pull too far out to one side instead of straight back toward your hip. His head will be pulled to that side, causing him to lose sight of the cow.

If your horse fights you when you sit down and pull back slightly on the reins, then pull harder. Don't jerk his mouth, but be very firm about what you are asking. If he responds, make sure to quickly release the pressure. But

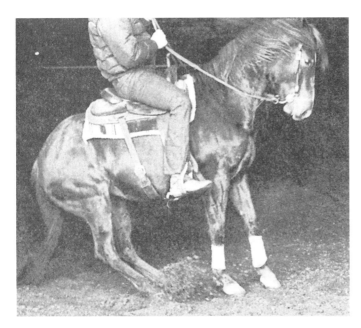

Stopping a horse from a lope. The rider has given his horse a signal to stop first by sitting more deeply in the saddle (without leaning back) and then by lifting the reins. His body position is good. To emphasize his cue, the rider uses his free hand on the reins to take up the slack at a lower point to discourage the horse from further elevating his front end. The result is a straight stop with the horse's rear end fully underneath himself.

if he still fights, use some psychology instead of brawn. Make him back up a few steps quickly each time you ask him to stop. Get him thinking about backing up instead of just stopping. It won't be long before your colt will sharpen up his response when your weight sinks down in the saddle and the reins lift from his neck.

> Body language, when combined with reins and legs, is how you communicate with your horse. I had trouble understanding exactly what it meant to "sit down in the saddle" until someone said to just "sit on your pockets and *think* stop." My horse then could anticipate what I was going to ask of him, and it helped me stay balanced and loose.

Everything happens faster when you ask a horse to stop from a lope, and your reaction time must accordingly be quicker. The sequence of cues is exactly the same, only now you've got to make an extra effort to sit down and relax your legs so that you don't brace against the stirrups or grip with your knees. Any stiffness will mislead your horse into thinking he should go faster instead of stopping.

Backing in a Straight Line

A cutting horse will be more precise in the way he stops when he has learned how to back properly. When he is able to bring his center of gravity over his hind legs with his weight evenly distributed on his haunches, as in backing, he'll be well prepared to move quickly forward or sideways to stay with a cow. If he learns early on to associate stopping with backing up, his reaction will be automatic when you ask him to stop: He will think *back* and will be in the best possible position for any subsequent move.

When asking a horse to back up, first use some body language by sitting down deeper in your saddle. Then evenly and steadily pull on the reins. If his hip moves over to one side, straighten him out with your leg (the best contact area for controlling sideways hip movement is almost a foot behind the cinch). If he is sensitive, you may need to use only the calf of your leg against his flank to straighten him out. Otherwise, press your spur into his belly until he moves away from the pressure.

Many trainers spend a good deal of time backing their horses and turning to either side, as well as backing in circles. These exercises strengthen a horse's haunches and legs and help him to be collected and balanced over his hocks.

Circles

Walking and trotting in small, even circles on a loose rein works a horse's muscles, creates flexibility, and helps him to position his legs. Such exercises also teach him how to bend in response to the rider's leg.

In a field or arena, ask your horse to move around an imaginary circle about 30 feet in diameter. Notice how he keeps his shoulders, rib cage, and hips moving in a slight arc or bend. Now take him in consecutively smaller circles, using a bush or another object as the center of the circle. Move him around this point as evenly and as close to it as possible. The tighter you make that circle, the more you'll have to concentrate on keeping the bend that you've created. Hold, or restrain the horse's forward movement if you need to slow him down, while controlling the bend with your legs. If he should throw his hip to the outside, you can put him back into correct position by pressing your outside spur into his flank behind the back cinch. Or if he gets out of position in the front end, you can hold his forward

Trainer Dave Hammond demonstrates circling a colt to get him bending and flexing his body correctly. He is directing the colt's nose by pulling lightly on the right rein. His upper body is relaxed and straight, his right hand is low and quiet, and his right leg is away from the colt's belly.

movement by pulling back on the reins, while simultaneously using your spur in the shoulder area to correct him. If he doesn't want to bend at all, press your inside leg and spur into his belly just behind the cinch. Remember that your legs are the primary steering mechanism for your horse. When you really need to direct his front end and nose, use the reins too, but only as an aid to your legs.

> Often I can see my own mistakes in other riders when I watch a cutting clinic or when I'm warming up at a show. Some riders use the reins too much while correcting their horses. I too have done this to my horse—inevitably, up goes his head, away goes his concentration, and out goes his understanding of what he's supposed to do.

Leads

When loping, a horse always *leads* with one shoulder, consistently advancing that shoulder and forefoot ahead of the other. When loping in a fairly small circle, most horses will naturally advance their inside shoulder to keep their balance. For example, a horse moving around in a clockwise direction will be balanced if his right shoulder and forefoot (and his right rear leg) are leading.

Although not too important during the initial dry work phase of training, correct leads can be critical to a horse's balance when he is working a cow, because often he must make very quick directional changes. The herd behind him is his pivotal point and he moves generally around them in a very slight arc. Thus he is in a better position to move *away* from the cow when she challenges him, because his shoulder is dropped *away* from her. Should his cow-side shoulder be incorrectly leading, he'll drop *in* toward the cow and cause a negative chain reaction: The rider's shoulder also will drop *in* toward the cow, causing the horse to compensate for this incorrect weight distribution by stepping closer to the cow. The result will be a slower, rounded turn (called a "barrel turn") instead of a quick and dynamic pivot over the hocks. His reaction time will be inhibited, setting him up to lose a quick-turning cow.

If your colt does not naturally take correct leads when you lope him in circles, he will most likely correct himself as soon as he begins working cattle.

> During dry work, there are two ways to help a cutting horse become accustomed to moving in a good working position. You can lope him a big circle on the correct lead while tipping his head and neck to the outside. Buster Welch says you can also lope a horse in a circle on the wrong lead to keep him from dropping his shoulder to the inside. This exercise tires the horse, and can help you take the edge off a nervous horse when you are warming him up.

Half Turns

A horse should be able to change direction by turning easily over his hocks in response to either the rider's leg or a cow's movements. When done properly, these turns will be quick and balanced, with the horse's head and neck in a natural, low position as he pivots on his back legs. This motion can be very dramatic when working a cow because the horse will drop down on his haunches as he stops. He then remains eye-to-eye with the cow through the turn.

Nonpro Dan Lufkin is riding a mare that has excellent balance when turning with a cow. She has her back legs well underneath her rear end, forming a platform from which she can turn in any direction. Correct body position when stopping is the key to these dynamic turns.

If your horse doesn't have a solid turn, examine the way he stops. Does he gather himself up so that his hind end is squarely underneath, almost as though he were going to back up? If not, you'll need to work on that, first by backing him up each time he stops until he naturally prepares to back up on his own. Does he pivot on his hindquarters, almost folding into himself, to move in the other direction? If not, check your own body position. Are you leaning in the saddle and anticipating the turn? Are you asking him with your leg to *complete* the turn? Are your reins even and not elevating his head? And, if he overturns, is your leg still pressing against his side when it should be *away* from it?

Riders often spend too much time working in a pen with no cattle, attempting to get a horse to turn correctly. All that really needs doing in dry work is to make sure he responds to your direction and that he will listen to you. He'll learn to handle his turns with agility as soon as he works a cow.

Watch other riders work cattle and observe the way each horse turns and how he uses his body. A turn that is rounded, instead of being a pivot over the hocks, is going to be slower, and may cause the horse to lose the cow. Chances are that the horse does not have a good stop, or that the rider is somehow using his body incorrectly.

Spinning

Spinning a horse, or turning him around on his hocks in 360-degree circles, isn't part of working cattle, but some pros feel it has its place in training. Spinning can help a horse be more accurate in the way he uses his legs. But this movement also puts more weight on a horse's front end, which is not to his advantage when he must stop hard and pivot in the other direction with a cow. Basically, spinning gets a horse thinking and listening to his rider.

To ask a trained horse to spin to the left, hold his forward movement by maintaining light rein contact, and simultaneously press your right spur into his belly just to the front of the cinch so that he understands he is supposed to move his front end instead of moving sideways. He should respond to you by pivoting around on his hind feet. If he is slow to react, zing him with your spur to get his attention. Then press him again in front of the cinch and keep pressure there until you are ready to stop. If he is spinning correctly, slacken the reins so that he can relax his head and neck. Spin him around a few times, then release your spur pressure. He should stop immediately. If he is slow to stop, counter his direction by pushing your other spur into his side.

If your horse travels backward or sideways instead of remaining stationary, you are doing something wrong. Riders who don't feel very secure in the saddle when spinning often will use the reins for balance. They pull too hard on the reins, causing the horse to back up instead of staying in place.

Again, don't overdo the dry work on a cutting horse. Remember that you are his coach, and the emphasis needs to be on helping him learn to react to a cow. Dry work such as spinning should be reserved for helping him coordinate his legs and brain so that he can have quicker reactions when in front of any type of cow.

7

THOUGHTS

ON

TRAINING

Training is how you go about conditioning your horse to meet the demands of competition. It involves working within a horse's mental and physical capabilities to prepare him for the cutting arena. Training is adding layer upon layer of new experience to a solid foundation. How fast a colt matures and how far he can be taken in the field of cutting remains to be determined: Each horse has his own ability level regardless of his rider's talent and expectations.

Buster Welch says of training, "I like to develop a cow horse first. If he does that, then I like to train a cutting horse, and then see if I can develop a contest horse out of him. When he starts knowing the difference between these, he's a good contest horse. Some of 'em will make a good cutting horse but won't be a good contest horse because they know they don't need to do some of those things that are really not necessary."

As soon as a colt has learned to move correctly and respond to his rider he should be introduced to cattle. Cattle are the primary teachers of a cutting horse, helping him to read and counter their moves until he is able to handle many different types with agility, precision, and confidence. Basically, your job as a rider is that of the copilot, ready to help whenever your horse is confused or makes a mistake. This job can be very demanding if you are to help your young student attain his highest level of ability. You must be, as Lindy Burch says, "correct, quick, and consistent" in the way you ride and in the way you train.

Although your own facilities and access to cattle will somewhat dictate the type of pens you'll to use, the optimum arrangement is a pasture and two or three enclosures of different sizes.* The best and most versatile areas for training are a round or oval pen somewhere between 120 to 200 feet in diameter, and a square pen that is about 100 feet wide by at least 120 feet long. By having more than one area to work in, the cattle tend to last a lot longer with a change in scenery and routine, and horses will learn more about cattle by working them in a variety of situations.

Training Goals
for Each Age of Horse

Two-Year-Olds

Because a colt's first impressions will be long-lasting, the two-year-old year is the time to concentrate on building his confidence, endurance, and interest in

---

*Because there are many methods used to train cutting horses, and because no one has a corner on the market, three training arenas—round, oval, and square—will be discussed in a sequence derived from observing and talking with several of the country's top professionals: Chubby Turner, Buster Welch, Bill Freeman, Lindy Burch, Mike Haack, and Joe Heim. My intention is to help explain the more popular ways cutting horses are trained, and to encourage experimentation. We're all students of this sport trying every possible way to help a horse learn to stay in front of a cow.

working a cow. There will be much repetition in stopping, backing, waiting, and reminding him to look at the cow in front of him. Because this is such an important time of development for your young equine student, you need to be patient without expecting too much.

> For the first two or three months, the well-known pro Joe Heim works his colts in a large round pen with one cow three to six times a week for fifteen to thirty minutes at a time until they show interest in watching and following a cow. He may then work only three or four days a week, teaching the basics of stopping, turning, and rating a cow. This schedule will vary, depending upon each colt's energy level and ability to concentrate.

Three-Year-Olds

Your goal now will be to build on this colt's early training by gradually increasing the demands on him with an eye toward the autumn futurities. Because he is physically ready, you can begin to quicken his reaction time to a cow. But take care not to push him to do more than he is mentally ready for: A three-year-old is still young, and only capable of learning a little at one time. The idea is to get him to an acceptable ability level just before the fall futurities, not two or three months early. So, for now, concentrate on building expressiveness and interest, and create more challenge by occasionally choosing tougher cows for him to work.

> Joe Heim rides his three-year-olds, depending on the stage they are at, three to six times a week for up to half an hour per session. He uses a variety of pens, and will begin to demand more from these colts as they progress.

As futurity time approaches in the autumn, you'll want to tune up your colt occasionally by emphasizing correctness and tightening up his stops and turns. If not overdone, this added pressure will be beneficial: Competition isn't far off and your colt needs to be exposed to small doses of precise work. If you haven't already taken him to other arenas to work cattle, or to local cuttings where you can ride him around or tie him in the warm-up pen, do it now. These are good ways to condition his mind for life on the road.

Four-Year-Olds

If you have a horse that can work cattle well and move with agility, it's wise to keep him in a consistent training program through his four-year-old year so that he will maintain the intensity and explosiveness you've been trying to build. He can take more pressure at this age because his mind has nearly caught up with his physical capabilities, but it's very important that he stays interested and alert when he works cattle. Vary the pens and the situations as much as you can, work two to four times per week, and emphasize the areas that need attention. But don't forget the basics: Solid stops and consistent position on a cow are the keys to making a good cutting horse.

Five-Year-Olds

Although a five-year-old is considered to be fairly solid or "finished," he still needs to be exposed often to cattle and pressure situations if he is to compete in the aged events. But a horse that knows the basics quite well can benefit from occasional breaks in routine such as trail rides or rounding up small herds of cattle.

Seasoned Horses

An older horse should know the rules, but you will always have to go back and school him to keep him honest and quickened up for competition. Concentrate on sharpness by insisting on good solid stops and precise turns. Avoid the tendency to work him on cattle every day simply because *you* need the practice. A horse needs to respect his rider and to like cutting cattle; he'll learn to cheat you or become sour with too much repetition. Freshen him up by taking him on trail rides, or use him as a ranch horse whenever possible.

> Keep your horse interested in his job. As Joe Heim says, this is done by "not overworking or making him hold an impossible cow."

A Sound
Approach to Training

Some points that may help you develop a good mental approach toward training a cutting horse are listed on the following page.

- Twenty or thirty minutes of training per session is about all a horse can take mentally. Have a plan of what you want to work on, and then use that time to your best advantage.
- Strive to develop a cutting horse's *natural desire* to work cattle. He was bred for this, and he will learn more from a cow than from his rider's constant interference.
- Try to be as correct as possible every time you ride. Remember that all bad habits begin at home: namely, with the rider.
- Be patient and flexible without becoming too critical of a young colt. Your pupil is an individual that has good days and bad days, just as we all do. It's important that he stays interested and that he tries.
- Never punish a horse in any way that will confuse him. He needs to know exactly when and where he did something wrong so that he can learn from it. Correct him as quickly as possible, then direct his attention toward the cow again.
- Chubby Turner is often heard telling riders to "keep it simple and stick to the basics, for cutting is only a game of 'left stop' and 'right stop.' " How easily we lose sight of this idea.

Many people attempt to train or correct a horse by copying what they see a professional do. But *seeing* and *understanding* can be very different. Whenever you observe other riders, remember that often they are reacting to situations that you may not even be able to perceive. A good rider will "feel" the beginnings of an incorrect movement and fix it before it has even become a problem, especially before it is apparent to an observer. So keep an analytical and open mind while trying to pick up pointers. Figure out why something was done, and ask if you are unsure or don't understand.

Preparation and Cool Down

Three phases should accompany every training session: getting your horse ready to be ridden, warming up to prepare his mind and body for physical exertion, and cooling down after you finish training. Don't overlook any phase if you want to avoid problems, for muscle injuries and soreness hinder a horse from improvement not only physically, but mentally as well.

Before You Ride

Check the equipment you will use. Make sure everything fits properly and is in good repair. A small piece of torn leather can lead to a serious accident.

Look over your horse when grooming and saddling him. Take note of anything unusual in the way he looks or acts. Check his legs for bumps or swelling, pick out his hooves, and put splint boots on his front legs. Some horses may also need their back legs protected with boots if they tend to hit or scrape themselves.

Well-known rider and trainer Don Dodge feels that it takes almost a year to condition a horse to the saddle. Toughen up his belly and prevent sores by loosely cinching your colt and tying him somewhere for an hour or so before you ride.

> Reining-horse trainer Les Vogt says that he checks "all of the gauges" every time he gets on a horse. That's something worth remembering.

Warming Up

There are many opinions about how to warm up a horse and how long the process should take, but the desired result is always the same: to be at the point where your horse is settled down and listening to you. You don't want him too fresh, but at the same time, he shouldn't be worn out from an overdose of dry work and loping.

Warm-ups loosen a horse's muscles, get his lungs in top shape, and keep his mind on business. For purposes of conditioning, warm-ups don't need to be long for a young colt. He'll build muscle strength while working a cow in situations where there is little chance of muscle strain. But further on in his training, he will be required to give maximum effort while working a cow. These warm-ups become quite important for suppleness and stamina.

> Whenever you warm up your horse, *ride* him. Some people will use a motorized Hot Walker or turn a colt out in a pen to run, but I feel that warm-up time is valuable and shouldn't be wasted. Get to know what your horse is like under saddle when he's fresh. *Listen* to him and learn to *feel* the slight changes in disposition from day to day. If he is nervous or charged up, you might trot or lope him longer than usual without even working a cow. Or perhaps he won't have any spark; you'll need to learn when to quit early so that he will be fresher the next day. Train yourself to listen, and you'll get to know each horse much better.

A typical warm-up for a colt in training begins by walking him around on a loose rein until he starts to relax and lower his head. Then ease him into a jog or lope, moving in large, even circles. Vary the direction, increasing the pace occasionally so that he uses different muscle groups. This may take anywhere from five minutes to an hour depending upon the horse and the situation.

When loping, tip your horse's head and neck slightly to the outside of the circle so that he bends his body in a way similar to how he will when working a cow. If he is especially high or nervous, he can also be loped on the wrong lead to help get the edge off; being on the wrong lead is more tiring than being on the correct one.

Once your horse feels relaxed, ride him in small circles in each direction to limber up his spine and get his legs moving quickly. Get him collected and listening to you by asking him to walk forward a few steps (or trot or lope if the horse is a bit lazy), then stop and back up straight. Remember to sink down deeper in the saddle when you ask for each stop. Turn him around over his hocks, and then back up again.

> Chubby Turner suggests a good way to find out whether your horse is warmed up: Spur him forward when you're loping. If the horse speeds up only for a stride or two and then slows down again, he's ready to work a cow. But if he continues on at the faster rate, ride him longer.

After you have warmed up, whether for training or competition, don't simply sit on your horse for an hour or so while waiting to work a cow. Dismount, loosen the cinch, and let him relax until it's almost time to cut. He will lose his mental freshness after standing still for a long time, and must be warmed up again for a few minutes before he works.

Cooling Down

Proper care is equally important following a workout. Wash off your horse's sweat with cool water and then scrape off the excess moisture. If the weather is too cold for a water bath, be sure your horse is rubbed dry with a towel. Look him over once more, checking his legs for any scrapes or swelling, and pick out his feet. Before putting him in his stall, walk him or put him on an automatic walker until he has cooled down and relaxed. Some trainers will cool down a horse and then tie him up somewhere for an hour or so before putting him back in his stall. This prevents him from expecting to eat just after he works, and it also keeps him from drinking large quantities of water following a workout.

Pasture Training

Cutting began in the wide-open spaces of the 1800s, when cowboys gathered and sorted cattle for doctoring and branding strictly by horseback. The best ranch horses in those days were "cow horses" in the true sense of the phrase: tough, smart, and hard-working. Today, cutting has become an arena sport. Cattle are confined by fences, and a horse must keep a cow separated from the herd in a highly pressured situation under a strict set of rules. Although cutting horses are now trained almost exclusively in arenas, it can help if first they learn about cattle by working in an open ranchlike environment. If you are lucky enough to have access to cattle and a pasture or a field where the footing is safe, two or three months spent gathering and sorting cattle will give your young horse a relaxed and ideal foundation.

> When I bought my first futurity horse from David Holmes's Arrowhead Ranch in Oregon, it was immediately apparent that this young colt was comfortable around cattle and ranch life. Almost every Arrowhead youngster is introduced to working cattle in the pastures and hills where they are ridden daily to gather and move cows to other areas. When talented trainer Kenny Davis takes over, these colts have a solid and unpressured foundation.

For the first several weeks, simply allow your colt to become used to being around cattle. Walk him slowly around and through them in the pasture. The cattle will probably be scattered around and grazing, so it should be easy for your horse to relax and watch them as he follows different groups.

Find one cow standing apart from the others, and walk your colt toward her. Just let him stand and watch her for a while. If he looks around and loses interest, tip his nose back in her direction. The cow will move when she becomes uncomfortable; this is the time to show your colt how to mirror her movements by stopping and turning when she does. He may become frightened if the cow starts to run or turn too fast. If so, back him away and find another cow.

Fifteen minutes every other day is about all a young two-year-old can take, so do not overdo these sessions at first. If he's worth anything at all, your colt will soon be watching cows with some interest and want to turn when they turn. Make this a game for him now, and don't pressure him to do any more than he's capable of doing.

Once your colt shows more interest in watching cattle, you can begin to drive a few cows a short distance away from the herd and then allow all but one to filter back. The remaining cow will eventually want to join the others. When she tries to go around you, your colt will probably attempt to turn and move with her. Show him that he can easily mirror a cow's turn by making complete, defensive turns, like a basketball guard giving ground by backing up a step or two each time he's challenged by an opponent. Help him to complete a left turn, for example, by pressing your right leg into his side.

A green-broke colt is perfectly capable of doing ranch work once he has had even a minimal amount of experience around cattle. You and he can drive cows from one part of the pasture to another, move them through gates into another pasture, and separate a few from the others. Keep in mind what you are trying to develop: a well-broke horse that is relaxed around cattle and that likes to work them.

8

THE

ROUND PEN

Cattle

Cattle vary greatly in temperament. They can change from day to day depending on the weather, how much they've been fed or handled, and their general state of health. They also have the dubious ability to develop all kinds of problems overnight. With these points in mind, *learn to know your cattle.* Look them over each day, sorting out the ones that need doctoring, and make a point of leaving behind those that appear run down. Determine which cows will work best that day and which ones should be avoided. (You should remember problem cows by the characteristics that you can see from your horse, such as coloring and distinguishing features of the horns, ears, tops of heads, backs, and tails).

> The real masters in cutting competition have spent a lot of time studying and learning cattle at home.
>
> A good cow to work is often the type of cow you'd like to own: healthy and well-proportioned, with a glossy coat and a kind eye.

To start colts on cattle, or to put the finishing touches on a horse of any age, trainers like to use well-built round or oval pens ranging in size from 100 to 200 feet in diameter. These large areas allow for a good deal of flexibility in the way a horse can be trained, and cattle seem to work better in them than in square pens or the smaller, more confining, round pens popular a few years ago.

> Buster Welch first thought of training horses in a round pen instead of a square one after he studied a diagram about the process of hearing that his doctor had given him. The diagram was drawn in a circle, and Buster began to think about all the relevant things that take place within that shape: Roundups are done in a circle, old corrals were always round, and cattle seem to flow more naturally in a circle. It followed, then, that training in a circular pen might be a better way to control the mad dash and panic that happen with cattle when they are in a square arena. Buster tried his idea when gathering cattle in Colorado. Later that year, he returned to Texas and won the Fort Worth Futurity.

A round pen initially is used to help build a colt's interest in moving with a single cow at an easy speed around the perimeter. As the colt progresses, he learns to read and react to a herd that is either in the middle of the pen or at the side.

> If you have only a square arena but would like to try working in an oval or round pen, it's certainly easy enough to put portable panels in each corner. You can also make one of the long sides into an oval shape by using panels.

Ideally, a round pen should have several gates spaced around the perimeter, each of which leads to an alley or a small holding pen for the cattle. Cattle that are brought into the pen from one gate and taken out another will not tend to "hug" one particular area and will be more likely to move around the pen.

Whether you work alone or with someone helping is a matter of personal preference, although it's often convenient to have assistance to make a lazy or sour cow move. When asking someone to help, be sure he knows what you're trying to accomplish and that he understands the training process. "Helpers" often become a little overeager to keep the action going at a time when just the opposite may be needed.

If you prefer to work alone, there are a few things you can do to help break up a cow's pattern of moving or to cause her to change direction. You can move your horse out and around to the front of a cow to make her turn in the opposite direction, or you can move around toward her hip and encourage her to go forward. In either case, back your horse a step first so that he knows he is taking directions from you. Otherwise, he may think it's okay to walk straight toward a cow anytime he feels like it. He's got to learn to be *defensive*, not offensive, with a cow. Another way to approach a cow is simply to *back* your horse around toward her front or rear end.

A cow's pattern of moving and hugging the fence can also be interrupted by setting up a few barrels or fence panels just inside the perimeter. Joe Heim and many other trainers use these obstacles occasionally, with good results. The other alternative is to use a good cow dog to move your cattle. Certain breeds such as a Border collie, Australian kelpie, Australian shepherd, or blue heeler can be valuable help when a cow needs to be moved.

Working a Young Colt On
One Cow Around the Perimeter

> Because a young colt will be started in a ring snaffle, hackamore, or a light bosal with a running martingale, you'll ride with both hands on the reins most of the time. Review the material in chapter 5 regarding rein use and body position. Both are important elements in helping your young horse build confidence in you.

When beginning to train your colt on cattle in an enclosed area, a 120- or 130-foot-diameter round pen provides you with a controlled environment where your horse can learn to rate a cow and mirror her actions. Cattle are

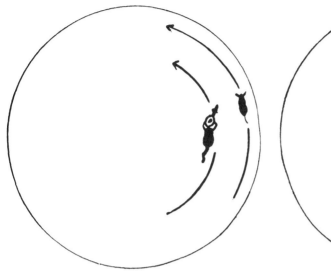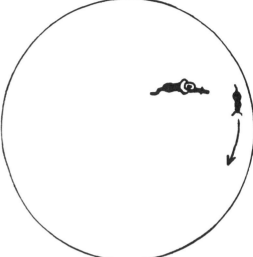

Starting a colt in the round pen. Teach him to mirror the cow's movements by keeping him parallel to her and slightly behind so that he can easily see her.

Walking toward a cow's hip to make her move forward along the rail.

fairly predictable in such a pen, for they'll move around the circumference and change direction without panicking. If they're fresh and haven't been worked, they will keep your horse interested by moving constantly and by watching him. The more times cattle are worked, the less interested they are in moving or responding to a horse.

> Bill Freeman prefers to start his colts in an outdoor pen. He thinks that they will have a better basis for concentration if they learn to watch a cow regardless of the many distractions. After two or three weeks, he feels, they will be better prepared for serious work.

Begin with only one cow in the arena. She will move around the perimeter trying to escape from your horse. You will be on the slower, inside track, mirroring her movements (see figure above left). At first, concentrate on helping your colt learn how to stop with the cow, turn when she turns, and match her speed (or "rate" her) as she moves around the pen. Get him interested in what this cow is doing by continually providing him with a cow to look at. Develop his natural instinct to "play" with an object (in this case,

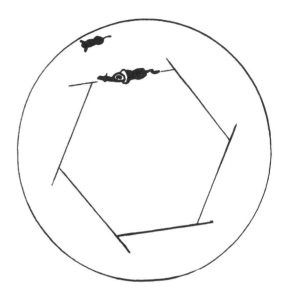

A hexagon within a circle. The cow is moving in a circle, while the horse mirrors her and learns to move in a hexagonal pattern.

a cow), and avoid interfering whenever he's watching or reacting to the cow. If you show a colt every single step, he'll begin to rely on you for direction instead of on his senses. And if you're too demanding, he can easily become confused or scared.

> When you are first learning about cutting, try doing this exercise on foot to get the feel of what it's like. A good amount of concentration is required to rate or synchronize your movements with a cow, and you'll quickly become intense. This intensity is what you should expect from your horse once he has learned the basics of rating.

As discussed earlier, when a cow is standing still and you want her to move, there are several ways to do it. When working an inexperienced colt with a short attention span, however, your top priority is to keep him in a position where he can *always* see the cow. Instead of backing him toward a cow, first teach him a consistent and direct way to approach her. Back him up a step, and then move your hands slightly forward on his neck while squeezing him with your legs and directing him straight toward the cow's hip. When you get just close enough to make her uncomfortable, the cow will start to walk forward along the rail.

The moment that the cow starts to move along the fence, tip your colt's nose in the direction the cow is moving, and squeeze him forward so that he turns and moves into a position parallel to her and slightly behind. He'll need

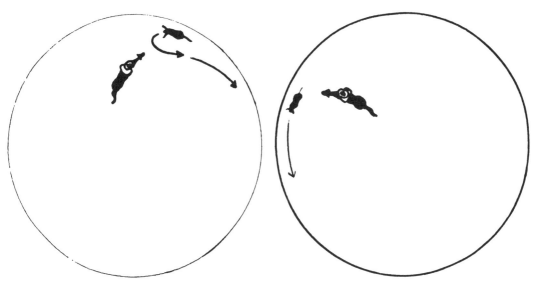

Walking around toward the head of a cow will not only help her to start moving, but it is a way to make her change direction.

Walking around toward the rear of a cow will force her to move forward in the same direction she is facing.

help to complete his turn, and you can do this by pressing him in the belly with your cow-side leg (the leg closer to the cow). The colt will then be far enough away from the cow at the end of his turn so that he can clearly see her without pressuring her. The distance should be anywhere from 5 to 20 feet, depending upon the cow. If the cow is afraid, you should stay farther away from her to avoid making her run too fast, but if she is slow, you can move in closer.

Tipping a colt's nose shows him direction, but forcefully pulling him around will take his attention away from the cow and onto you. He needs to learn to read the cow, to know when and how fast to turn by reacting to *her* instead of to you.

Don't rush your colt's turn. Help him to start it if he doesn't do so on his own. Use your cow-side leg to make sure he finishes, but let him find his own particular way of turning.

The position that a young horse should maintain while rating a cow around a pen is quite important. Trainer Mike Haack best analyzed correct position as looking like a hexagon or octagon within a circle. The colt will move in a series of straight lines while the cow moves around the perimeter of the circle pen (see figure on page 70). When moving forward, make sure that your colt can always see the cow by keeping his head directly across from her hip. As soon as the colt's line of travel starts to intersect that of the cow, or when your colt moves ahead of the cow, hold (or check) the colt's forward movement. Simultaneously, press him in his side to move him away from the cow. Then let him begin rating her at a new angle. Should the cow stop or turn away, back your colt up a step and then wait for the cow to move again. If he loses interest while moving or standing, back your colt up a step and turn him to face the cow by rolling him over his hocks. Then walk him toward the cow's hip to start her moving and create more interest.

Rating a cow by moving in straighter lines is becoming popular among trainers because so much can be accomplished in a short amount of time:

- By moving in straight lines, pausing, and then changing angles whenever the position on a cow needs adjustment, a colt learns not only to respond to his rider's leg, but to watch and respond to the way a cow is moving. This is great preparation for the way he will work from a herd.
- When a colt learns to maintain a position where his head is directly across from the cow's *hip*, he can always see her and thus will have more time to prepare for any move she'll make. He has a point of reference that allows him time to think. This gives him confidence. If he lags behind, or trails, a cow, the cow will be forced to move faster, and the colt will naturally want to chase her. Conversely, if he's allowed to move farther ahead than the cow's hip, he'll lose his working advantage when she turns and goes the other way.
- A colt that learns to pause and back up a step when a cow gets too close to him assumes a defensive posture. This posture helps draw a cow in toward him instead of driving her away.
- Because the colt will learn to stop and back up a step every time the cow stops or turns away from him, it is unlikely that he will ever step out toward a cow. Instead, he has learned to gather himself over his hocks in preparation for any fast movement.
- Most fundamentally, a colt learns to watch the cow. If his mind wanders, the rider is there to redirect his attention.

Be ready, especially in the first few days of training, to slow your colt down to a stop whenever the cow begins to do so. Don't make him stop abruptly, even if the cow does, but do let him get an idea of what this game is all about. If he goes a little beyond the cow in the process of stopping, just circle him around toward her to force her to turn, then put him into position parallel to her when she moves in the other direction. The next time, if you can stop him at the same moment the cow stops, quickly back him up a step and then loosen the reins. Let him relax and look the cow. Standing still will be his reward. He can catch his breath, relax a bit, and learn to wait.

This two-year-old colt is allowed to lower his head while the cow is standing still. He is relaxed. His rider will let him remain in this position as long as he continues to pay attention to the cow and will react when she moves.

A relaxed horse often will lick his lips, play with the bit, lower his head, or point his ears forward. Each of these movements means that he's not worried about his rider.

When a moving cow turns to go in the opposite direction, concentrate first on stopping your colt straight. Then, if he needs assistance in turning, tip his nose in the cow's direction. Let him turn on his own, and ask him with your cow-side leg to get back into position. Although a young horse will make mistakes, he needs to figure out how to handle himself and to turn correctly. This will happen as soon as he realizes that his job is to stay in position with a cow.

Some people feel that a young colt should turn over his hocks when changing direction with a cow. However, this pivotal, more physically demanding turn takes time to master and should not be hurried or forced. A hard turn can frighten a colt, cause him to stiffen his neck and brace against the bit, take his attention off the cow, and make an incomplete turn. Let him find his own way of turning for now, and concentrate instead on correct position.

Cows differ in the way they move and respond to a horse. You'll best help your colt by choosing cows that he can handle (not wild or belligerent individuals) and by manipulating them to do what you want them to. Like people, cows have an area around them in which they feel safe. Buster Welch describes this area, or space, as a "bubble." You can often control a cow's speed and direction by figuring out how big her bubble is, and then move to where you are just at its very edge. If you invade a cow's bubble by moving in too close, she will escape. If you move slightly away from her bubble, she will slow down.

A young colt needs a lot of time to think about the cow and about his job. Don't ask him to work any closer to a cow than is necessary to keep her moving. Figure out the distance you should be from each cow in order to avoid causing her to run too fast, and then try to maintain that distance as you rate her around the pen.

When it's obvious that a cow is not going to move after a minute or two of standing, there are a few methods to get things going again if you have no one to help. First, back your colt up over his tracks for just a step or two, then press him around over his hocks so that he's facing the cow. Walk him slowly toward her hip until she moves and then ask him to get into position again. Another tactic is to back a step and then circle your colt around to the front of the cow. The cow will probably turn and move the other way, almost inviting him to go along. Either way, the cow will not only be the one to teach your colt how to turn, but she'll keep him interested.

Be sure to walk toward a cow *only* when she is standing still so that your colt learns early to stay in position and rate her whenever she's moving.

You'll feel a little bit of resistance from your young horse after a few days of asking him to walk to a cow's hip or around toward her front. This means that he has just figured out the cow will move again and that he'll have to make a harder move in order to stay in position. Your colt is starting to think on his own and to become a little bit cautious, and it's a great moment when you feel this reaction. Let him stand and watch the cow for a minute or two. Slacken the reins if he lowers his head. This is a perfect time to reward him for doing well by quitting that cow.

Don't walk to the head of a cow if your colt shows he's unwilling to do so; you run the risk of letting him discover he can scare a cow away by lunging toward her head. A smart horse will figure out how to avoid work if given the opportunity.

Once you feel resistance from your colt when you ask him to move toward the cow, try another method. Circle him around toward her tail. Although he may do this for the first few times, it won't be long until he figures out that *any* move toward the cow will force her to move. At this point, if you were to squeeze his sides slightly, you'd feel his body tighten up almost to the point of trembling, his concentration fully directed toward the cow. From now on your tactics for getting a cow to move should change. Either ask a helper to move the cow for you, or back your horse around in a big circle to the point where he causes her to move, and then put him into position.

There always seems to be one cow in every bunch that moves in only one direction, regardless of how many times she has been around the pen. When this happens, don't try to change her course by walking slightly ahead of her because you'll be asking your colt to get out of position. Concentrate on correctness as your colt learns to synchronize his speed with the cow's and move in straight lines. And keep yourself intent, even if the one-way scenery becomes a little boring: Your horse will pick up your attitude. Then, when you've had enough, find a time to quit when the cow has stopped, and go get another one.

There are different philosophies regarding the use of reins to direct a horse. Some trainers depend on their reins much more than others and get good results. The best advice I've heard is to be aware of overuse and misuse, because too much rein work can take a horse's mind (and head) away from the cow. Over-reining can easily irritate a horse or hurt his mouth. Try to let him learn as much as he can from the cow. Remember that the only time he should be told what to do is when he's *out of position.*

There will be times when things can progress quite well for a number of days, and then suddenly nothing seems to work no matter how hard you try. This happens to every person and to every horse. All you can do is be consistent in your approach and think hard about what *you* are doing when things aren't coming together. Most important, maintain your composure: Anger on your part will really upset your horse.

Problems

Typical problems that arise during the first stages of training include:

- Chasing something is a natural instinct for horses. It's *not* natural for them to stay back and wait. Therefore, if a cow runs away or cuts across the pen, don't chase her; simply stop your colt and start over by walking toward the cow's hip again. Remember that we're trying to teach a colt how to *rate* a cow, not rope one! The next time this problem happens, think about your position and whether it was correct at the time the cow ran. Chances are good that you may have allowed your horse to be a little bit behind her hip.
- A colt may want to get too close to the cow as they move around the pen. Teach him early to respond to your leg and to move away from the cow when you ask him so that you can maintain a constant, almost parallel distance from the cow. Think of this as like having a tight rope that connects your horse's nose to the cow's hip.
- A colt may tend to come in toward the cow at an angle as you slow down for a stop. If you allow him to do so, you will put your horse *ahead* of the cow where he can't see her. This can leave your colt in a difficult position if the cow turns suddenly, because he won't be able to make such a hard change of direction. It will also prevent him from drawing the cow *toward* him, which will become quite important later on in his training.
- If your colt continually goes beyond a cow that stops, there are a few corrections you can make:

  - Hold your cow-side rein a bit tighter so that your colt's head is always slightly directed toward the cow (you can also hold both reins in just your cow-side hand, switching hands each time he turns).
  - Let him go past the cow, then tip his nose toward her and circle him around to her front (or rear if she has already turned). Keep your spur in his sides until he has caught up with her again.
  - Monitor your position on the cow, making sure you are on her hip. When she stops, don't walk toward her head or shoulder to start her moving. Instead, walk toward her hip.
  - Be sure that you are looking at the cow, not at your horse. You must focus all your attention on the cow if you expect your horse to do likewise.

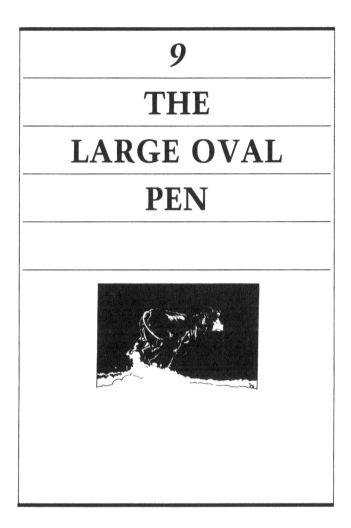

9

THE

LARGE OVAL

PEN

A large oval pen that measures about 120 by 160 feet offers many additional training benefits. Not only is a change of scenery important for a colt, but the extra space allows him to move with more speed as he rates a cow. Also, cattle used several times in one round pen will be more likely to respect your horse and to cooperate if put in another, larger pen. The more you can confuse them, the longer they'll move around on their own without someone else in the pen helping you. And, of course, the more *natural* that cattle are in their movements, the easier it will be for your colt to learn how to "read" them.

Working One Cow
Around the Perimeter

Start just as you did in the smaller round pen, with only one cow. When the cow moves as your colt walks toward her hip, he should take an immediate interest and turn to go with her, especially if he feels your intensity and concentration. If your colt turns and moves with the cow, leave him alone until he needs some guidance. However, if he's not interested in her, remind him with your leg that his job is to get into position about 15 to 20 feet away (depending on how much pressure the cow is comfortable with), with his head across from the cow's hip. Again, your colt's position at the cow's hip is to his advantage because he can see her clearly at all times without having to turn and face her. He will also draw the cow in *toward* him instead of pushing her away, thus creating more eye-to-eye contact between horse and cow. If the cow moves too fast and scares him, increase the distance between them, or get a calmer cow to work.

Some people train "head-to-head" or even farther forward (or "long") on a cow. The idea is to let the cow see an opportunity to turn the other way quickly and get back to the herd. As a result, these riders feel, she will "carry" the horse with her as she turns, teaching him to make the big sweeping turns often seen in competition. This sounded logical to me at first, but it puts a lot of pressure on a horse, especially a young colt. Not only will he lose his point of reference (the cow's hip or shoulder, depending upon his level of training), but it may cause him trouble with his turns and with his ability to stay in position on a fast-moving cow. A colt is neither physically nor mentally ready to stop and turn quickly enough, while an older horse may lose his interest in a cow altogether if he is pushed to do too much.

As you move your colt in fairly straight lines around the pen with a cow, concentrate on position. Using the same concept as in earlier training, move in a hexagonal fashion while the cow moves around the perimeter of the pen. Anytime your colt gets farther ahead than the cow's belly, hold his forward movement, adjust your angle on the cow, and then move forward again to keep him in position with her. Maintaining these imaginary lines requires precise leg work on your part, because a colt may still veer off from the line you've chosen.

> When correcting your colt, don't take his attention away from the cow. Use your legs or reins to reposition him quickly, then let him go back to work. Be sure that he knows his job is to watch the cow.

Whenever the cow stops or moves *away* from your colt, stop and quickly back up a step or two in order to shift his weight onto his hindquarters and get his hocks positioned underneath his body. Then release the reins to let him relax and lower his head again to watch the cow. This exercise helps the colt prepare to move quickly forward or in the opposite direction in response to a cow. And, because *cutting is built around a solid stop,* repetition in early training helps cement this well-balanced "ready" position before the colt works with faster, more aggressive cattle.

> When you ask a colt to stop and back up, first give him a chance to stop on his own. Help him only with your own body language (sitting down deep and forcing more weight onto the saddle). Then, if he needs further reminding, pull firmly on the reins and back him over the track that he just made.

If your colt loses his attention, repeat what he has already learned in the smaller pen: Back him a step, roll him over his hocks, and walk straight toward the cow's hip. Another technique is simply to let him stand, hoping that the cow will move and attract his attention. (A helper or a good turnback dog can be useful here.) If the cow does move, however slightly, your colt should move with her at the same speed, staying in position. Show him that he has to do only as much as the cow does, not more. As Mike Haack says, "It's the little bitty moves that are going to become the big moves later on."

Turns also require occasional review. When a cow makes a slow, unchallenging turn, your colt should respond by making a complete, 180-degree turn. Should he not finish it, help him to do so with your leg. However, he won't have time to make as full a turn if the cow turns aggressively. Avoid the tendency to hurry a young colt through these faster turns. Make sure that he stops quickly and can see the cow, but let him turn on his own and at his own speed. (If you try to rush the turning process with your leg, you may make your colt step *toward* the cow.) Then help him to complete his turn so that he can stay in position with the cow.

Once your colt is accustomed to working in this larger pen, expect him to become more intense. He will start to look for, or "hunt," the cow and to focus on her for longer periods. Your own concentration and reaction time are key factors in maintaining his new intensity level. For your part, think straight lines, and think stop. Lower your rein hand onto your colt's neck when he's working well, and encourage him to do as much as he can on his own. Create the *desire* to work a cow.

When either checking a horse's forward movement or stopping him completely, be sure that he can always see the cow. Some trainers hold the reins in their cow-side hand so that when they pull it back the horse's head is not pulled away from the cow. The reins must be switched from hand to hand whenever the horse changes direction. It is a good exercise, and makes a rider aware of the slightly off-sided impact he can have on a horse's head whenever he pulls back on the reins with one hand.

As training progresses and your colt is mentally capable of more challenge, change the way you work. Quicken his reaction time by making it tougher for him whenever he is out of position. Use your spurs more forcefully to "tell," instead of "ask." Mix up his routine occasionally. Instead of standing and waiting for a cow to move, back your horse around in a big circle and get him thinking about using his hind end. Confuse him so that he doesn't become mechanical in his pattern, then put him back into position on the cow again. Also, you can work a faster cow occasionally to see how your colt handles her. He may not stop as well as you'd like, and he may round his turns slightly instead of pivoting in the other direction by correctly using his hocks, but remember that your student is still very young. Give him some space to learn from his errors.

New and talented trainer Ben Patterson said that he learned the importance of changing the way one works a cow from Mike Haack. Mike spends a good deal of time backing a horse around to get a cow moving instead of walking forward toward her. When the cow does move, he just puts his horse back into position on her. This helps to break up patterns that horse and rider adopt when they work cattle.

The reins are crossed over and held in the rider's right hand so that when he pulls back, the colt's nose will be tipped slightly to the right.

The reins are now held in the rider's left hand to ensure that the colt's nose will be tipped to the left so that he can see the cow.

Every so often when your colt is moving with a cow, test him by squeezing his sides to see whether he will walk ahead of her (thus moving out of position). If he shows unwillingness to do so, by lowering his head down or turning in to face the cow, don't force him to move ahead of her: He is doing a good job. As a reward for this behavior, quit working the cow and let him relax for a minute. If, however, the colt forgets and walks ahead of the cow (this will happen occasionally), circle him back in toward her, then use your spur firmly to put him in where he is supposed to be.

Quitting a Cow

To "quit" means to stop working a cow. Whenever you've decided to change cows or to stop for the day, do so just as you will later in competition. Stop by pulling back slightly on the reins while simultaneously putting your free hand on the colt's neck. He'll quickly learn that this signal means he did a good job, for you've allowed him to relax and catch his breath. Timing is very important here. You should *only* quit working a cow when she has stopped moving or has turned away from you. And never let a colt stop working a cow unless you give him this signal.

When you quit one cow with the intention of working another, stop correctly, then turn your horse around on his hocks in the same direction he would be turning if he were still working that cow. This teaches him that he can never turn away from a cow until he has first turned toward her.

If you are finished working for the day, get off your horse as soon as you have quit the cow. Loosen the cinch and remove your colt's splint boots. Never quit and then ride out of the arena, for your colt may mistake that as meaning that he can leave anytime a cow stops.

Problems

- If your colt is still not stopping crisply, either when you ask for a stop or when he is responding to a cow, back him up a few steps every time he stops. Be firm and very quick, but without jerking on the reins and hurting his mouth.
- When a colt doesn't turn well in one direction, walk to the rear of a cow and let her "pull" the colt through his turn. She will teach him to turn; all you need to do is help him finish the turn with your leg and then spur him to catch up with the cow.
- A colt that continually wants to be long (to go ahead of the cow) should not be allowed to do so. Being long often forces a cow to turn away from your horse, pulling him in toward her. The result is a rounded

turn and a loss of working advantage. Stop your horse early when a cow stops, and walk him toward her hip whenever you want the cow to move. Make him catch up to the cow instead of being ahead of her.

Working a More Experienced Horse

Working a more seasoned horse in the round pen with one cow is an effective training method because it takes him back to the basics. Not only does this method provide variety from the horse's normal routine of working in a herd, but it's also a good way to correct any bad habits that he may have picked up.

Work your horse just as you would work a colt: Move in straight lines and maintain position at the cow's belly. Regulate ("check") the horse's speed and alter the angle in which he moves when he gets too close to the cow or goes farther ahead than her hip. Stop and back up a step whenever the cow stops or turns away. These little, yet very precise, moves will help make his stop crisper. He will also be reminded to keep a correct distance from the cow instead of shouldering in toward her. Should he get out of position or lose interest, don't babysit him as if he were a colt. Make it *hard* for him. Put him into position by using your spur. If he moves just slightly ahead of the cow, stop him, quickly turn him over his hocks with your spur, and then turn him back to where he again faces the cow. Be fluid; make it happen so quickly that he barely realizes what happened.

> In response to the feel of the reins lifting from his neck and a spur pressed against his side, a trained horse will turn over his hocks. This response may come in handy during competition if he should forget to turn with the cow.

Working with a Group
of Cattle in the Center

When a colt is more experienced, to the point where he cannot be coaxed to leave his position on a cow even when squeezed by your legs, change the way that you work him. Don't allow him to depend on the same unpressured, one-cow situation every time he is schooled. A very popular way to use a large round pen, especially when there are no fresh cattle available, is to bunch up a small herd (from five to fifteen) in the center of the pen. Separate one cow, then work her as you would in earlier training. You'll now be teaching your colt to walk into a group of cattle, drive several toward the fence, and then separate one and prevent her return to the herd. Although you can easily work alone here, it's convenient if someone else keeps the cattle grouped in the center and helps start a lazy cow moving.

To settle cattle in the center, put a bale of hay in the middle of the pen for them to eat. Then warm up your colt as you move around them at a trot or a lope, being careful not to disturb them as long as they stay in the middle. If they wander off to one side, move them back toward the center again and continue riding around them until your colt is warmed up.

> When top pros warm up a horse in preparation for working cattle, everything they do has a purpose. "Long-trotting" (an extended trot) helps a horse relax and move low to the ground, whereas loping helps quicken the heart rate and loosen leg muscles. Often a horse is loped in a circle with his head and neck tipped slightly to the outside to simulate the body position used when working a cow. To get a horse thinking *back* and listening to the rider, a pro will exaggerate the way he sits down deeper in the saddle and lift the reins slightly. Instead of just stopping, the horse must respond by sinking back on his haunches. If he doesn't do so immediately, he will be asked to back up 10 or 15 feet.

Once the cattle are settled, walk slowly into the group. Let your colt get comfortable in the midst of them, for he may be a little nervous if he has never stood in a herd (which will not be the case if he was "started" in a pasture situation). Then ask him to walk toward several cows and drive them all the way out to the fence. To do so, aim at the shoulder of a specific cow and walk your colt forward until she moves away. Aim at another, and then at a third, until you have gained control of a few cows and can move them away from the others. Then push the cattle slowly forward, keeping them together and controlling their direction by moving behind them in a zig-zag fashion.

- In order to make your horse move in a zig-zag manner, use your legs as if they were steering wheels.
- Drive at least three cows because two can often be difficult to separate.
- Never let him walk *toward* only one cow. He should learn that one cow in front of him means to stop and get to work.

Once your cattle are under control at the fence, slow down or stop until they begin to get restless. If they just stand there, "sneak up" on them by

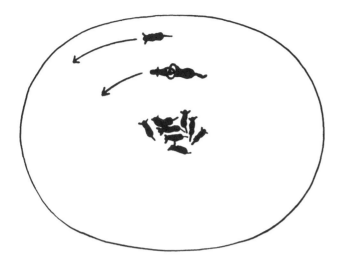

**Working from a herd that has
been settled in the center of
a pen.**

urging your colt forward one step at a time. Look for one cow that seems to
want to remain near the fence. To separate her and keep her under control,
aim your colt straight toward the cow's "control point," somewhere between
her hip and her shoulder. You need to figure out where to aim your horse in
order to prevent the cow from moving. If the cow suddenly turns and runs off,
single out another that you think will stay. Then ask your colt to wait and
watch this one while the others wander back to the middle.

Separating one cow from the others is an art in itself. Because you're just
beginning to introduce your colt to herd work, concentrate on finding a cow
that does not panic when she is by herself. Don't make it hard on your colt by
choosing a wild cow that wants to run away.

As soon as only one cow remains at the fence, back your colt a step or
two and let him look at her. When she decides to move, or when you step
toward her hip, you'll work in the same manner as before, concentrating on
correct position (colt's head across from cow's hip) and working in straight
lines while rating her.

The cow will try to return to her buddies grouped in the center. She will
move with purpose, challenging your colt instead of trying to get *out* of the
pen. To prevent her from reaching the herd, keep your colt in position with
her just as you did in earlier training. But when she tries to get past him,
teach your colt to give ground by pressing him *away* from the cow with your
cow-side leg. This will put him in a better position to guard the herd and
reduce the confrontation. As a result, the cow may not challenge quite so
forcefully.

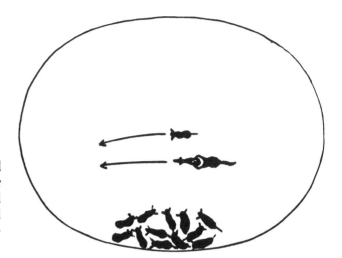

This is how to work a herd at the side of an oval or round pen. They are settled in the "pocket" that is formed by the slightly rounded fence-line.

The combination of your helping a colt to stop and turn correctly and the colt himself becoming "cow smart" will cause quicker stops and turns to occur naturally. Let your colt become more fluid in the way he uses his body by offering him repetition and consistency, while you correct only such major errors as incorrect position on the cow.

Problems

- A colt that becomes too excited or afraid when moving with a fast cow is bound to make some errors. Try to avoid these mistakes by increasing the distance between you and the cow, or else stop when you can and find a slower cow. Also, use a large pen if possible so that cattle feel less pressure. Otherwise, use only one cow in the pen at a time and work around the perimeter as in earlier training.
- A stop that isn't up to par needs to be dealt with right away. Review your colt's way of stopping, and find out where it is that he needs help. If he is not stopping or backing up straight, one of your legs may be pressing against him at the wrong moment. If he doesn't gather himself onto his haunches each time, be more consistent in backing him each time he stops.

Working a More Experienced Horse

A more experienced horse should be asked to rate a cow at her *shoulder* instead of at her hip or belly. This position is harder because it requires more exact timing and accuracy in his stops and turns, with less margin for error. It is excellent preparation for arena work because it helps a horse perfect a harder stop and a full, sweeping turn.

Working from a Herd of Cattle at the Side of the Pen

When you feel that your colt has developed confidence in how he works a cow around the perimeter of the pen, put him in a situation that will bridge the gap between what he can already do and what he will need to learn to become a finished cutting horse. That involves working from a herd of cattle at the side of your pen. Instead of rating a cow around a full circle, he will now be covering less than half that area, learning how to *hold* one cow away from the others in a semicircle. His way of moving will be much the same as in earlier training: in a fairly straight line as he goes back and forth across the pen. However, his stops and turns will be frequent and demanding, and his position on the cow must be even more precise. Working from a herd at the side of a pen is quite similar to cutting competition, although without the same pressure.

Because you still have a very young student, you'll need to adapt to his particular ways and avoid pushing him to do more than he can. As Bill Freeman says, "Gear your training to his needs and his attention span." Some two- and three-year-old colts may require more time to mature than others, occasionally needing as much as two extra years to achieve the foundation necessary for handling the pressures of cutting. Be sure that your goals are realistic for your colt.

You won't want a helper pushing a cow back toward you now unless your cattle are sour and refusing to move. At this stage, a colt needs to learn more about the natural movements of cattle instead of false ones prompted by a helper. It will also be good practice for you to drive a few head of cattle a long way and to control their speed and direction by yourself.

Warming Up

Preparation becomes more important when working a horse under tougher conditions, so your colt will need a longer warm-up before you ask him to move faster. He has already built up his muscles and lungs during early training, but stops and turns will now be more stressful to his legs. Take the time to long-trot and lope for a minimum of fifteen minutes before you ask your colt to cut a cow, and extend this warming-up process as he advances to harder moves in the coming months.

Before You Begin

Before you start, settle a group of cattle at the side of your training pen. A group can contain anywhere from five to fifty head, depending on cattle availability and on how many cows you want to have in your arena. Many people have a herd of about twenty head, but they may only use one-third of them in a day.

To settle the cattle, watch where they want to be after you've brought them in. Most likely, they will stay by the gate where they entered, especially if there are other cows just outside. But they also may want to settle in another area. Where they are doesn't really matter in a circular pen as long as they are grouped together and standing along the fence.

Walk, then trot back and forth in front of the herd. If the cattle are fresh, it may take a few minutes to bring back the strays and show them that they will not be bothered as long as they stay together. During this process, pay attention to your own horsemanship and to the way your colt is moving. Make sure that he stops correctly when you sit down deep in the saddle and raise the reins slightly, and that he turns over his hocks in the other direction when you hold and then press him in his side.

Entering the Herd
and Bringing Out Cattle

When ready, slowly walk into the herd. Keep your hand low and hold the reins just loose enough to allow your colt to relax. As always when training, be sure you hold your reins in a position that gives you control, but not so tight as to affect the way the bit hangs in your colt's mouth or where a bosal hits his nose. Stand quietly among the cattle as you survey them, deciding which ones you want to use and which ones to avoid.

Using your legs to direct your colt, move behind four or five cows and begin to push them away from the others. As they move forward, one cow will be out in front and is called the "lead cow" or "point cow." It is this cow's direction and speed that you must control in order to bring the rest of the cattle along more easily. Should another cow move up and take her place (which can happen many times in the course of a minute), simply change your focus to maneuver the new leader toward the opposite end of the pen.

This colt is being urged to look directly at the cow standing in front of him. The rider has lifted the reins as a signal to move forward toward the cow, and his legs are squeezing the colt's sides. The result is intensity. The colt is "locked on" to that cow.

Cows that are more likely to be potential leaders are often the ones at the edge of a herd. Keep an eye on them so that you'll be ready to move behind the new one as soon as she takes the lead. Drive them far enough from the herd that you have enough room for working and giving ground to a single cow.

Trainer and top showman Bill Freeman feels that everyone should learn to cut cattle on foot before attempting it on a horse. I tried it and found, after having exerted a good amount of energy separating and driving cattle (and losing a few too many), that every single movement I made became much more calculated. The job of figuring out how to get a cow from point A to point B became my sole focus. And so it should be on horseback, whether you're starting a colt or cutting a cow in the Fort Worth arena. Plan, maneuver, manipulate, but separate a cow from the others with *finesse.* Although you're bound to come up with some wrong decisions, if you learn how to make good cuts at home, you'll soon be picking up a check in competition.

Setting Up for a Cut

As soon as the group of cattle you have separated begins to get restless, start looking for one cow (often one of the lead cows) that wants to stay out.

Maneuver her so that she stays in the center of the arena and stands still when the others leave: Quietly control this cow by placing your horse between her and the others, facing straight toward her (cutters call this "staying in her face"). If she happens to be facing you, don't stare straight into her eyes because it makes a cow so nervous that she may take off at a run.

As soon as the cow is alone and you are certain that the colt is facing straight toward her and watching her (his ears will probably be pointing her way), lower your rein hand onto his neck. You'll encourage your colt to develop *intensity* in the way he watches a cow by positioning him correctly and by relaxing the reins. Squeeze him slightly with your legs. You'll feel him tense up. He may even lower his head so he is almost eye to eye with the cow, ready for any move she makes.

If you *think* slow and calculating, you'll produce a horse that does the same.

Moving Across
the Pen with a Cow

You've already prepared your colt to move in a series of straight lines while rating a cow around a pen, and to slow down or stop and change angles when he moves beyond her hip or when she turns away. Now he will learn how to apply these actions in front of a herd with a cow that is likely to challenge him more often. In order to play her game and stay "connected" to the cow in front of him, your colt must be ready to react. The cow may turn away from him, or stop, or turn in toward him right in the middle of the pen; or she may go to the fence and challenge him there, or stop and go the other way.

- If the cow turns away from him, your colt will know from his earlier training to stop straight, back up a step, and watch her. He will have the advantage because he is not chasing after this cow; he is being defensive, guarding his territory in front of the herd.
- When a cow just stops still, you should *already* have "melted down" into your saddle. Bill Freeman says that sitting down deeper forces more weight onto the bottom of the saddle, which cues a horse to stop and get set up on his haunches. Your colt should stop correctly. He may then want to turn and face the cow. This is acceptable as long as he does not step toward her.
- A cow that turns *in* toward your colt somewhere in the middle of the pen is challenging him and trying to return to the herd. This is the type of cow that every cutter wants to have when competing because she

Horse and cow are facing off in the center of the pen: every cutter's dream. The rider is Dan Lufkin.

keeps a horse busy and can make him look like a superstar. Unless she happens to be an "alligator" (a very tough cow that a young colt should not work) and can outmaneuver him, make your colt face her squarely and hold his ground. He can be aggressive and hold such a cow; much like a basketball guard who is looking for a good opportunity to steal the ball away from an opponent.

• When a cow tries to dive in toward you on one side of the pen or the other, which is often the case, give ground so that she doesn't press quite so hard. This is also a way to get your colt set up to defend his ground in a better position. Again, as in basketball when the player with the ball moves down the side toward the basket, the player guarding him backs up to set up a better block.

• A fast cow that stops in her tracks and turns quickly in the opposite direction will be tough for your colt to match, especially at first. If she is too fast for him, *forget about the cow and concentrate instead on your colt's stop.* Make sure that he is correct and straight before he begins to turn. If the cow is now heading the other way, turn your colt in her direction and catch up with her. Or quit and get another cow to work. Don't make your horse hold a tough cow if you are not accomplishing anything by it.

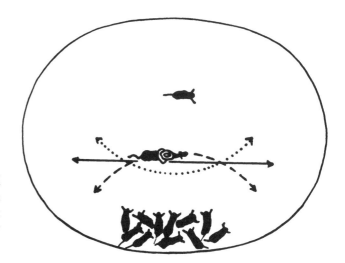

Different patterns are used to hold a cow and prevent her return to the herd. Don't get locked into using only one of these.

People seem to lock in to different patterns when they ride a colt across the pen with a cow. Some feel that a horse should work only in an arc, giving ground to a cow on either side. Others insist that a horse hold a straight line on any type of cow, whether it be sour, wild, or a nonmover. Still others like to work only in an inverted arc. But each horse has his own level of ability and way of reacting to a cow, and each cow differs in her manner of moving. Be adaptable! There are times to be aggressive and "hold" a cow out in front of you, and other times you will need to back off and "reel" her in toward you. Let each cow teach *you* something, just as she'll teach your colt.

Stopping or Turning a Cow

There are two ways to persuade a cow to stop or turn:

- When moving toward the *side* of the pen, slow your colt down and use your leg to press him away from the cow. The cow will then be more likely to stop, or will at least try to come in toward you (instead of being frightened away). You will also have put your colt in a better position to turn when the cow changes direction.
- If you are in the *middle* part of the pen with a fairly agreeable cow, push your colt slightly ahead of his normal position so his head is even with her neck. The cow will then be more likely to stop and turn the other way. If her turn is not too quick, your colt will be able to stay in position with her, countering as well as controlling her. You may be

tempted to push your colt even farther ahead than the cow's neck, but resist. You never want him to think he can be that far out of position. Save the more aggressive moves for competition situations when you can ask him to step farther forward and take control of the cow.

Quitting a Cow

As I've said, quitting is an important part of cutting, a way to establish good habits—or bad ones that will haunt you during competition. Many riders forget their job when they quit working a cow. Each time you quit, be sure to do so for a reason. And do it in a way that reinforces something your colt should already know.

- Quit when you feel that your colt is not able to hold a tough cow.
- Quit when the cow is standing still or turned away from you instead of challenging or running across the pen.
- Quit near the middle of the pen instead of near the fence, because it shows that you are the one who's in control of the cow. Otherwise, the fence is influencing where the cow stops.
- Give the same signal every time you ask your colt to quit a cow. Pull back slightly on the reins while placing your free hand on the horse's neck. Turn him over his hocks in the direction he would move if turning with a cow, and then turn back toward the herd

It is often easier during training to stop working a cow at one side of the pen instead of in the middle (quitting in the middle takes work). Do so only as long as you quit correctly and turn your horse back toward the middle of the arena before returning to the herd. A bad habit will quickly develop if you quit when your horse is facing the fence and turn back to the herd without first bringing him over his hocks toward the middle, as if he were working a cow. Once a horse learns he can quit and just turn away from a cow when she is at the side fence, he will do it again. I've seen this happen during competition, and it's a lost entry fee every time.

If you haven't already done so, now is the time to give your colt some "road seasoning" by taking him along when you go to cuttings. Show him the sights: Ride around the arena, and tie him to a fence in the warm-up pen where he's out of the way but still can watch the goings-on for a few hours. And if the cutting event has a practice pen, you can pay to work your colt on cattle for a few minutes.

Problems

- *Rushing turns.* Stop sooner, making sure that you do not allow your horse to move farther ahead than the cow's hip. Hold him off with your cow-side leg to keep him from turning in toward her. You might also try holding the reins in the hand that is farther away from the cow. This prevents you from inadvertantly pulling your horse toward the cow whenever you lift up on the reins.
- *Running off to one side.* Try some reverse psychology: Encourage your colt to move ahead of the cow if he has a tendency to do so. Then, once you turn him around, put pressure on him by using both spurs to move him back into position on the cow.
- *Creeping forward toward a cow.* Again, use psychology: Drive the cow as far away from the herd as you can, and then make your horse work hard when the cow pressures him. The cow will probably challenge him as long as he refuses to give ground. She will teach your colt to back off and give her some room; she will teach him about reacting defensively.

Working a More Experienced Horse

As long as a more mature colt or horse is mentally ready, you can increase the training pace and demand more. Keep him on his toes and make him think a little harder about his job. Although he should always be protected from too much running and from constant pressure, he can take some surprises. Teach him to challenge a cow when she asks for it, to control her without scaring her away, and to stop her in her tracks by utterly disarming her.

There are several ways to build the quickness and intensity your horse needs to advance in his training:

- When rating a "normal" cow (one that doesn't stampede across the pen or run right through you), ask your horse to maintain position across from her neck instead of her belly. He will have more control over the cow in this position, and he will also have to take more responsibility for her actions.
- Separate and drive several cattle to the opposite end of the arena before making a cut. There, your horse is in territory where he's not quite as sure of himself. When you make a cut this far away from the normal working area, your horse is more likely to assume a defensive posture

and to *hunt* the cow because he knows she'll be coming at him every chance she gets. He will develop "the look," the expression of readiness that is so appealing to spectators and judges.

- When you've cut a cow and she is standing still, urge your horse to step toward her. If he is worth his salt, when he feels your legs squeeze his sides he'll do all he can to keep from moving a step toward her. If there's anytime he is likely to show expression, it's here. He might bow his back, lower his head to watch the cow more closely, paw the ground, or squat down on all fours so that his belly is almost touching the ground. Don't overdo this extra pressure on any horse, however, because you can just as easily take all of the expression right out of him—permanently.

- Instead of setting up for a perfect cut every time, occasionally surprise your horse by walking toward the herd and quickly taking the first cow that pops out. Wake him up, and put him on his guard. Try to keep just one step ahead of him—just as he should be one step ahead of the cow.

Correctness in your own body position becomes even more important when you are working harder and moving faster. As you progress through the many steps of training, try to refine your own movements so they become as fluid and natural as your horse's. And whenever something goes wrong, look to yourself first and try to figure out how you can do things better.

An older horse needs *reward* just as much as a colt. When he's "cowing," or concentrating fully on a cow, leave him alone even if he stays in one place for a minute or two. After he has worked hard, let him relax and catch his breath before cutting another cow. And when he has done a good job, stop right where you are, get off, and loosen the cinch for his reward.

10

TRAINING

IN AN ARENA

Regardless of age, any horse will benefit from being trained, if only occasionally, in a large square pen (also called an arena). This configuration causes cattle to feel more pressure, run faster, and be more determined to return to the herd than an oval or round pen. They'll tend to run back and forth, not only trying to return to the herd or the gate they entered from, but also diving for the safety of the corners. As a result, a horse must maintain perfect position on a cow at an often faster rate and for a greater distance in order to prevent her from reaching any part of that fence.

Trainer Chubby Turner feels that an ideal training arena is approximately 100 feet wide and at least 120 feet long, with a gate in the center of each side. Not only will these four gates help prevent cattle from hugging one particular area, but they provide more options for training. You can use the circumference, or the shorter, or the longer sides to train and to correct certain problems that a colt may have. And because cutting competitions are held in square pens, you can easily simulate competition in this arena.

> In most bigger competitions, the back fence is slightly rounded. This deletes the corners on either side of the herd, and forms a slight pocket for them to stay in while one cow is being worked.

Many trainers feel that using the sides of a square pen for training creates an artificial learning situation for a colt. They think that the fence, and not the cow, will dictate his movements and reactions. Be that as it may, there is merit in examining the many ways a square pen is used. The more you learn about different training methods, the better you can judge what works best. Change and experimentation are positive: Don't lock yourself or your horse into a specific pattern of training.

Starting a Colt

When starting a young colt in a square pen, round off the corners with fence panels and use it just as you would an oval pen. Work one-on-one around the circumference. Then put five to ten head of cattle in the middle of the pen and work around them.

Working a Cow Against the Fence

A colt will learn to rate a cow in a straight line and for a long distance when you train him to work one cow along the entire length of an arena. If there is a gate in the center of that side, a cow will be drawn toward the gate instead of always trying to hide in either corner. She will also stick closely to the fenceline instead of challenging and pressuring your colt and trying to go around him.

To begin, bring a cow into the arena through the center gate and let her move along the back fence as she tries to find an escape. Position your colt in the middle of the arena at a point where he can directly face the cow. If she

Working a cow against a straight fenceline.

does not move, back your colt a step (to get him thinking *back*) and then use your reins and legs to urge him to walk straight toward her hip. When the cow moves, your colt should turn and move in the same direction. His position should be exactly the same as in the round pen: parallel with the cow, about 10 to 15 feet away from her, with his head directly across from her shoulder. If the cow stops and your colt loses interest after standing in position for a long time, back a step, roll him over his hocks so that he's facing the cow again, then walk him toward her hip.

Good legwork on your part is important, for a rider's legs are the primary mechanisms for reminding a colt to keep his body in a straight line when he stops or moves with a cow. Use your legs as if they were your only means of steering or directing a colt. If he needs to move farther to the left when rating a cow, for example, press him in the right side with your leg. This way, you will avoid pulling his head off a cow by using the reins to move him over.

Working a Colt
Along the Fence with One Cow

A tougher situation occurs for a colt when you ask him to work against the fence instead of the cow (as above). He must not only defend the entire fenceline from a challenging cow, but he has nowhere to retreat so that she will slow down. He must move at her exact speed and stay in position on her shoulder in order to prevent her from reaching any portion of the fence. Working in this manner will sharpen a colt's reaction time. The fence insures that he makes straight stops, complete and precise turns, and that he moves

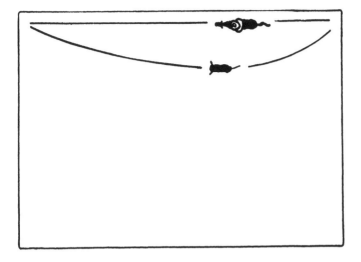

Working a horse against a straight fenceline is a technique used to build a horse's confidence in "holding" a cow instead of giving ground to her. It is also a way to ensure full, 180-degree turns.

in a straight line. It will also give him confidence in his ability to hold a tough cow.

It is best to have at least one helper to start a cow moving and then prevent her from hiding in one of the far corners. If you have no help, back your colt a step and then ask him to walk toward the cow's hip. The moment she moves, your colt should react by getting into position parallel to her with his head directly across from her shoulder. Whenever the cow challenges him, help your colt fade backward so that soon he is working very close to the fence.

> Work your colt in this way only when he is physically *and* mentally ready for the added pressure. An aggressive cow can be a real challenge to a colt's mind, timing, and ability.

A two-year-old colt is not quite ready to react consistently and stay in position on a cow that makes frequent and quick directional changes. You must, therefore, help him stop correctly and make complete, 180-degree turns when he is unable to do so on his own. This requires that you read a cow's every move, mentally anticipating each pause, stop, and turn. You should sit the saddle in a balanced position, knowing when to sink down and stay quiet and when to intervene by using your legs or reins. The faster things become, the more correct and automatic your reactions need to be if your colt is to learn how to maintain balance on every cow.

This colt wants to "shoulder in" to a cow, moving toward her instead of maintaining position. To correct this, the rider crosses his reins over and holds them in the hand that is closer to the fence. This way, the horse will be unable to turn his head (or shoulder) in toward the cow when she stops. When going the other way, the rider simply changes hands so that his fence-side hand is always on the reins.

The following situations may arise when training your colt on the fence:

- Your colt is late in stopping and the cow has already turned and is moving away. Simply help him to stop correctly and make a complete 180-degree turn. Then hustle him back to the cow.
- The cow remains in one place when your colt is late in stopping. Stop and hold him there. Then very quickly press your spur in his belly and roll him over his hocks so that he is facing the opposite direction. Just as quickly, roll him back to where he is face-to-face with the cow. This maneuver will quicken him up and make him think hard before he goes past the cow again.
- Your colt stops short in anticipation of the cow's turn and moves out of position. You were not quick enough to correct him. If he starts to slow down too early, quickly push him forward with your legs to where his nose is across from the cow's head. Exaggerate his position on the cow by pushing him slightly farther ahead than normal so that he cannot stop early.
- Your colt makes incomplete turns. These are easy to spot and correct when working against a fence. Find a less aggressive cow for your colt to work and concentrate on making him finish each turn. Every time he is more than halfway through his turn, press your cow-side spur in his belly, keeping it there until he is parallel to the fence.

When you're working in the pen in this fashion, two ways to handle the reins help a horse maintain correct position on a cow:

- If your horse wants to lean in (or shoulder in) toward a cow instead of working balanced and straight, hold the reins in the hand farther away from the cow (your "wall-side" hand) and switch hands on the reins after each turn. Then, when it's necessary to pull back on the reins to check your colt's forward movement or to ask him to stop, you will be just slightly tipping his nose in the direction of the *fence* instead of toward the cow.
- If a horse's timing is off and you want to be sure that he can always see the cow, hold the reins in your cow-side hand. When you need to pull back or stop, his nose will be turned slightly toward the *cow* instead of the fence.

Working a More Experienced Horse Along the Fence with One Cow

The difference between working a colt and a more experienced horse along the fence with a cow is one of position and pace. Regardless of the type of cow you use, a seasoned horse should make every effort to maintain position and hold the cow for as long as you ask him to. Regardless of his more advanced level, however, never ask him for too much at one time. Constant pressure from an aggressive, fast-moving cow is a quick way to take the desire out of any cutting horse. And remember that you are still in the process of training. Try to avoid mistakes, but don't scare or sour your horse by demanding more than he can give. And reward him by quitting when he has done a good job, even if it's only after five or ten minutes.

Using the Arena's Length to Drive Cattle

An effective way to use a large square pen is to drive five or six head of cattle to the far end of the pen, then separate one cow and ask your colt to fade backwards each time she challenges him. This exercise requires no outside assistance and will accomplish a good deal for horse and rider.

Asking your horse to drive a few head of cattle a long distance is excellent practice; it is difficult to do, especially when the cattle are not fresh. Much like playing a game of pool, you must plan ahead to control

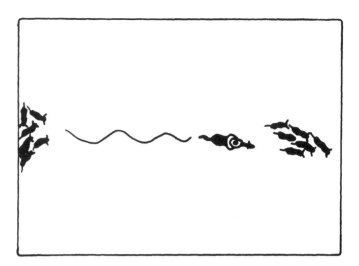

Use the entire length of an arena to drive the cattle and control their direction.

speed and direction. Because cattle often do not cooperate and tend to panic when they become insecure, you must learn to be calculating while driving them up the arena. The farther they are from their safe spot on the back fence, the more pressure they feel and the tougher they are to drive. Your horse will also feel this pressure because he knows he has to protect himself. He'll become cautious as the cattle begin to churn; he will lower his head and pay close attention to them. Reward him by feeding out more rein if he drops his head down, for this is precisely the behavior you want to encourage.

Separating a cow from the herd can be tricky no matter how far away they are from their "safety area." Most cows will panic when they discover they are alone, so your horse must be alert and ready for action the moment he sees only one cow left standing in front of him. When you are ready to make your cut, face your colt straight toward the cow you want to cut. Get the cow under your control while she is standing still.

When a cow turns without actually trying to get around your colt and back to the herd, your colt should hold his line. But each time the cow actually challenges him, he should become slightly defensive and give ground to her. Because the large arena allows quite a bit of space to continue retreating backwards, you can reinforce this defensive behavior on a horse with aggressive tendencies. Ask him to finish each turn and fade back by pressing him hard in the belly with your cow-side leg. Because you are retreating from a cow, you are giving the cow room to advance; you are simultaneously drawing her toward your horse, which keeps him interested.

This diagram shows how to work from a herd of cattle that has been settled in the center of the long side of an arena. A horse must cover quite a lot of ground to prevent a cow from gaining the advantage.

Using the Arena
Length with a Herd of Cattle

Using the entire length of your arena to hold a cow away from a herd of cattle introduces your colt to a situation resembling competition. However, there will be more ground to cover and no one will be standing in the corners to discourage a cow from diving in and hiding there.

Bring five to ten head of cattle into your pen from a gate in the center of the long fence. Let them settle by that gate before moving through them, so that they learn where "home base" is. Then enter the group and bring four or five away from the fence and out toward the middle. Before separating one from the others, be sure you are far enough out in front of the herd. In order to avoid being pushed back into the herd when working a cow back and forth across the arena, you must now step out and hold your line instead of letting your colt fade backwards each time a cow challenges him. This maneuver requires good timing and quick legwork on your part.

Working from a Herd,
Simulating Competition

You will better understand the finer points of riding and training a cutting horse after you work in a situation resembling competition: riding into a herd of between fifteen and fifty cattle, driving a few away from the others, making a cut in the center of the arena, and then preventing the cow from returning to the herd. Training in this manner (and with at least two helpers) is ideal for putting the finishing touches on any horse and readying him for competition. It's where all of the steps are put together—for horse *and* rider.

Working from a herd can be as challenging as you want it to be, depending on the type of cow you cut and the ability of your helpers. However, at this juncture you are still *training*, still in the process of building a colt's confidence and desire to work a cow, and still correcting him when he needs it. Don't push him too hard. As Joe Heim says, "There's no easier way to take the 'cow' out of a cutting horse" than by overwork. If *you* need the practice, then work a herd on foot or find another horse to ride.

> Also, as preparation for competition, read and reread the NCHA *Rule Book* and *Casebook*. Attend a few competitions so you can see the sort of performance that earns a winning score. Watch videos of the champions—every cutting horse magazine advertises them and they are well worth purchasing. And ask for advice or direction from other cutters who are qualified to give you good answers. Many well-intentioned people are ready with their opinions, but you can best learn from someone who has a winning record and a good reputation.

Settling Cattle

To settle cattle at the center of the back fence, bring them in from that center gate and walk back and forth in front of them so that they learn to stay there (to properly settle cattle for competition, see chapter 11).

Helpers

Although you can simulate competition without helpers, it is much easier (and often more productive) to have at least one or two riders helping you. The ideal, of course, would be to have four: one on each side of the herd, and two that are positioned out beyond where you will work. If you are lucky enough to have helpers, be sure that they know what you're trying to accomplish before you begin work. They should keep a cow moving as long as your horse is in position and working well, but back off whenever you are correcting your colt or having trouble with a tough cow. This is valuable training time, and you'll want to avoid having to give instructions when trying to

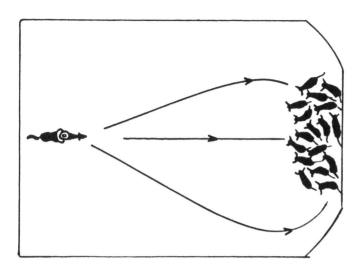

Different ways to enter a herd.

focus on the job at hand. (For a complete description of the job of each helper, see chapter 11.)

Entering the Herd

There are three basic ways to enter a herd of cattle: from either side close to the back fence, at an angle, or straight down the middle. It will pay off to practice all three methods, and from both sides, so that you are comfortable entering the herd from any direction. This versatility also benefits your colt. The more accustomed he is to being around a herd of cattle, the more relaxed and responsive he will be.

First, ask your corner helpers to bunch the cattle together at the center of the back fence. Adjust your reins so they are even and without much slack so that you can easily correct your horse when needed. Then, slowly approach the herd in one of the following ways:

- Down either side, entering the herd fairly near the back fence, is a popular way to begin work in competition because it assures the judge that you have made your required "deep cut" into the herd. Being deep in a herd gives you an opportunity to look over the cattle and manipulate the ones you want or don't want to bring out. Also, when cattle happen to be sour or "sticky," you should enter deep into a herd. The cattle will stay together and you can drive them farther this way, thus allowing you more time to filter through and pick out one to cut.
- From a 45-degree angle is the most popular approach, and a good method when the cattle are fresh or wild and you want to avoid going

in too deep and scattering them. You can also satisfy the deep-cut rule by moving your colt behind four or five cows. Because the cows that are the better cutting prospects are often more curious and stand out toward the front of the herd, you can easily scoop off a few of them without disturbing the others.

- Straight down the center is an approach that divides the herd. Splitting a herd by walking through the middle stirs up cattle that hug the back fence. This way, you can often flush out a fresher cow or one that has not been worked. If you decide to enter the herd down the center, alert your corner people ahead of time so that they can bunch the cattle together and help you push them away from the fence. Let them also know that whichever portion of the herd you turn toward is the portion they are to help you bring out to the middle of the arena.

Bringing Out Cattle

Enter the herd slowly so that you have time to look the cows over and get a feel for them. If you've worked these cattle before, you should know each one well; but if they're new to you, spend time figuring out which cows will be best to work. You needn't be a cattleman to pick a good prospect, but you must be observant.

You should learn how to handle "problem" types of cattle so that you can become experienced in dealing with them too:

- *Sour cattle.* Cows that have already been worked more than a few times are difficult to bring away from the back fence. Ask your helpers to bunch them together and then move with you to drive most of them forward. Because these cattle will be eager to return to the herd, be ready to block seven or eight of them when they start to turn and run toward the fence. Keep enough out in front of you (they are happier in a group) until you can get set up in a good position to make your cut.
- *Restless cattle.* Nervous or restless cattle require a quiet horse and good planning if they are to be brought away from the back fence without stampeding. Enter the herd slowly. Let them become accustomed to your horse for a moment, and then carefully push a few away from the herd. These cattle will not go far before they panic and take off in all directions: You need to be alert and ready so that you don't lose all of them.
- *Slow or "sticky" cattle.* Slow-moving, lazy cows will probably not work well. And cows that crowd closely together will be difficult to separate. When you see either of these types, ask one of your herd

holders to help move them toward the back fence. Then get behind the better prospects, sorting through them as you drive them forward.

Start to "shape" a few cows by getting *behind* the ones you want to bring away from the herd. Slowly begin driving them toward the center of the arena. Keep the lead cow under your control (aiming your horse at her shoulder), regardless of the number of cattle standing between you and her. If another cow takes her place, get behind the new leader. You should be able to do so on your own with little problem by now (with helpers, this job is fairly simple).

As you continue driving the cattle slowly forward, some of them may peel off in one direction or other. Don't panic when this happens: Keep your eyes on those you want to cut, and concentrate on controlling their direction and pace.

You are now approaching the area where the cut will be made, and you must decide whether the distance between you and the main herd is sufficient. Look behind you. Will there be enough room for your colt to work without disturbing the herd? Will you have space to fade backwards and give ground in case your colt is pressured by a tough cow? If you need to drive out farther, will the cattle allow it, or are they too restless?

There should be no difference between the way you manipulate cattle toward a certain spot in a fenced arena and the way you would do this on the open range. In the old days, if a cowboy was told to separate fifteen head of cattle and bring them to a certain spot for doctoring or branding, he would have a lot of work on his hands if he could not do it. The cattle would be spread out all over the area, and the cowboy would be looking for another job. In present-day competition, you will receive credit for making your cut in the center of the arena. This also is the best way to prepare your horse for balanced and centered work.

"It's better to cut a bad cow good
than a good cow bad."
—WELL-KNOWN CUTTER SAYING, ORIGIN UNKNOWN

Making the Cut

The way you set up to make a cut is the most important aspect of training and showing. Your colt's first turn with a cow must be correct: in the center, in position, and explosive. Here is where you help him establish his pattern of moving and his dominance over the cow. Practice making good cuts at home, whether on foot or horseback, until it becomes natural for you.

Holding the reins just tight enough to maintain light contact with your colt's mouth, sneak up closer to the cattle in front of you. Sense whether they can be maneuvered farther forward or whether they are feeling the pressure and are ready to panic. It's your choice whether to cut what you can now so as not to lose the entire bunch, or to continue setting up a particular cow.

If you have your eye on a certain cow that is not in the front, there are two ways to set her up to be cut. If she's grouped with the other cattle, sneak up toward her shoulder and try to drive her to the front of the group. If, however, she is uncooperative, stay on her shoulder and try to control her while the others filter back toward the herd. This technique may not work, in which case you should quickly move behind another cow before they all take off and leave you with none.

This is when you have to be subtle. You don't want to commit to a cow until you *know* you can get her separated. Be a good poker player: Have one or two "hole cards" in mind.

Holding a Cow

Your colt knows by now to start working as soon as he sees only one cow in front of him. But don't drop your hand down onto his neck until you are certain that he's "hooked" and moving as you want him to. Remember that his entire run is influenced by the correct timing of that first stop and turn.

The way to move when rating a cow in an arena is really no different than in an oval pen. You'll still be working in a fairly straight line, changing the angles in reaction to the way the cow moves. But now there are corners and sides for a cow to head toward, as well as a herd behind you. Concentrate on maintaining correct position all the way across the pen, and think about your stops.

> Bill Freeman talks about "bottoming out in the stop." This is not only a technique that you want to train for, but it's an *attitude*. It is body language that transfers directly to your horse. From the time you bring a colt into your training program until the time the buzzer sounds to signal the end of a competition, you should be thinking about "riding for the stops." Your sinking down deep into the saddle helps your colt come to a balanced stop and prepares him for any subsequent move. Anticipate each stop as though it were the most important part of your run.

Working different types of cattle will give you the experience necessary to become automatic yet flexible in your actions:

- If the cow you chose is wild, running from fence to fence or back and forth in a big arc, all you can do is rate her and be defensive. Keep your colt in position on her hip so he can see her at all times, and don't let her pull your colt out toward her. This is not the type of cow to be aggressive with unless she wears down and becomes workable, so play her game. If she challenges you when she moves toward the side of the pen, change angles and fade back slightly. Release the pressure on her. But if she goes all the way to the side fence and then tries to come in toward you, meet her challenge. If instead she turns away when nearing the fence, stop your horse and use your cow-side leg to move him away from her in the hope of drawing her in toward you again.
- A cow that challenges your colt in the middle of the pen will keep him interested and on his toes; this is the most appealing situation in riding or watching a cutting. Help your colt stay absolutely balanced with her, but allow him to find his own way of turning to counter her actions.
- With a slow-moving cow, simply let your colt mirror her stops and turns. Mike Haack says: "Don't ask your horse to do any more than the cow. If she makes a little move and your horse makes a big one, he's not mirroring that cow." Insist on absolute correctness when you are training. You can make fancier, more dramatic moves during competition.
- A cow that has a pattern of turning away from a horse instead of toward him is also a challenge, and one that should be practiced at home. Every time she turns away or moves away, ask your colt to stop, or pause, before he changes angles or turns. Get him thinking defensively so that she does not pull him out toward her and gain the advantage. Again, this pausing and changing of angles is just how you worked in the round pen.

Quitting

As in any other portion of training, be decisive and clear every time you choose to quit working a cow. Think about the perfect situation in which to quit: when you have stopped the cow in the center of the pen and she is just standing there bewildered, unable to make a move in any direction. And remember competition rules: Your quit must occur only when the cow is stopped, obviously turned *away* from you, or behind where the turnback horses are located. Stop working just as you practiced in the oval pen.

More Advanced Horses

When training a more experienced colt or horse, focus on correcting problems and helping him improve his timing. To be successful, you must stay very aware of his range of ability, and accept his own particular style of moving and reacting to cows. He's still a student, regardless of age. He will continue to progress if you can keep him alert, interested in his job, and in top condition.

Some areas that typically might need attention are:

- *Driving cattle from a herd.* If your horse becomes too aggressive when you are driving cattle up the center of the arena, slow him down by setting him on his haunches whenever he acts up. Or approach this in a direct manner by teaching him *why* he should be more cautious. Urge him to move farther up the arena than normal before you make your cut. Find a fairly aggressive cow to separate from the others, then insist that he stay in position across from her neck and hold her out there. Don't let him give ground as she challenges him. This is difficult work, and something he will not want to do again. In a sense, you're letting him have his way, then showing him how hard it can be.

  A horse that hesitates to drive cattle forward may be sour and overworked, or scared because he has been pushed too hard, or he may lack the necessary confidence because you've been exposing him to too many aggressive or sour cattle. He may be trained in the same way as another horse, yet respond quite differently. Take him back to basics. Build his confidence by working cows that he can handle, and help him find *his* level.

- *Separating a cow.* A more experienced horse will sometimes get too eager to cut a cow, either by focusing his attention on only one cow or by dancing around in anticipation of a cut. Both actions mean that he's not listening to you, perhaps the result of your permissiveness or because you are putting too much pressure on him each time you get set up to make your cut. If not taken care of in the training pen, this type of behavior will show up again in competition.

  Be certain to maintain *light* contact with the reins as you guide your horse toward being focused and centered on the cow that *you* want to cut. Drop your hand on his neck only after you are satisfied that you have his attention. Devote training time to working solely on driving cattle and making cuts, without even working individual cows.

- *Controlling a cow.* A more experienced colt should be able to move with and control most cows by staying in position across from their necks, instead of their hips or bellies. If you plan to enter such a colt in competition in the near future, you should spend more time now controlling a cow in the middle portion of the arena, trying to prevent her from reaching either side of the pen.

Chubby Turner compares this more advanced work to the way a cow was driven toward the branding fire in the old days when there were no fences to control cattle. If a cow turned suddenly and bolted for the hills and the rider didn't respond immediately, he'd end up chasing that cow until she ran out of air. In your situation, be aggressive in the arena's middle portion by holding ground, and keep the cow trapped there. Ride hard toward each stop. If a cow doesn't respond but makes a beeline for the side fence, slow down and rate her. She has the advantage, and the best you can do is give ground to her and try to draw her toward you. If this maneuver doesn't work and you have to go all the way to the fence to prevent her from getting back to the herd, then get aggressive again and hold your ground.

> Controlling a cow does *not* mean pushing a horse out ahead of her to make her turn. Consistently asking your horse to be this aggressive takes his normal point of reference away from him and forces him to make very hard turns. Keep him correct when he is in training and reserve this type of aggressiveness for competition, where you'll have ample opportunity to "hang him out there" when you find the right type of cow. It will be there that you can occasionally push him beyond a good cow and let him make those eye-appealing big, sweeping turns.

• ***Developing intensity in the stops.*** If your horse is the slightest bit late stopping with a cow or doesn't stop crisply, stop him hard with a strong pull and back him quickly. Then put him into position with the cow just as quickly. To develop intensity in the way he stops, catch him the moment that he has made a mistake, and point it out. Then leave him alone so that he has a chance to correct himself without your intervention.

Tuning

"Tuning" a horse means asking him for exactness and sharpening his edges. To some people, tuning means putting on the pressure, asking a horse to go *ahead* of a cow to force her to turn and then to make hard, sweeping turns.

Dan Manning is simulating competition. He has his reins looser than normal for a training situation because his filly has been working well. When she lost her concentration on a slow cow and needed to be corrected, Dan used his right hand to take up the slack from the loose reins so that he could quickly correct her. This way, he avoided pulling up on the reins and elevating her front end.

But to most trainers, tuning means tightening up stops and turns and quickening a horse's reaction time so that he's not defensive. It means emphasizing the basics.

Tuning a Colt

Tuning a younger horse is done at different stages of training in order to test his behavior and progress. It's also done just prior to competition. Although you may need to emphasize different points with each horse, keep the whole picture in mind when you're sharpening him up. Don't forget the basics of staying in position on a cow. Because tuning is hard work, it can whittle away at a horse's desire to hold a cow if it is overdone. Once every few weeks for five or ten minutes is sufficient.

When a colt has been on cattle for three or four months, try tuning him to find out how he handles the extra pressure. Tighten your reins slightly, and ask the colt to *hold* a cow (instead of rating her) by moving him farther forward so that his head is across from her neck instead of back at her hip.

Stop him a little shorter and quicker than normal, and move him through his turns with authority. Without overdoing this, find out how the colt reacts to the pressure and what his limits are. Get into his mind.

If your colt doesn't respond well to tuning or becomes scared, just train him normally for a week and then try again. Slowly build him to the level where you can tune occasionally without problem. Then, when futurity time comes around, you'll have a good idea of what he can take.

Tuning a More Experienced Horse

Work with a more mature horse in the same manner as with a colt but with more rider authority, because this horse already knows where he should be on a cow. Ask for a quick stop, and then clean up his turns by holding him just short of making complete 180-degree turns. Make him watch the cow and think hard about each move he makes with her. Insist on his attention for five or ten minutes and then leave him alone.

Many riders will tune a horse several times prior to competition and again for about an hour before they show, if practice cattle are available.

11

THE

ROLE OF

THE HELPER

Cutting and working a cow in competition require five people: the cutter, two riders who stay in either corner of the arena to keep the herd under control, and two riders who create the competition between horse and cow by pushing the cow back toward the cutter. It is a team effort, one that requires an unusual combination of respect and trust between a cutter and the four people whom he chooses to help him put together a winning run. These people are often some of his toughest opponents, and are riding in the same class as he is. In what other sport does this occur?

If you are relatively new to the sport of cutting, it's unlikely that anyone will ask you to help them at a show. Most competitors ask the more experienced riders, who know cattle and competition. However, it's quite important for a novice to understand the intricacies of helping *before* going into competition. Not only will you learn about each helper's particular job in relation to the cattle and the cutter, but you will know what to look for in a helper and be able to choose people who will do a good job for you. The more insight you gain, the better prepared you'll be to accept the responsibility for driving and shaping cattle, making a cut, and holding one cow away from the herd. Helpers can influence your performance, but ultimately, it is up to you to show your horse.

The job of a helper requires professionalism, honesty, respect for your fellow cutter, good communication, and cow sense. It asks that you put 100 percent of your effort into helping someone win, even though it could mean a loss for you if you are competing in the same class. Trainers and nonpros make the following suggestions about the role of a helper:

- You cannot be useful to another cutter if you don't know how to make a good cut yourself. You must also know how to hold a cow in the center of an arena.
- Respect the wishes of the cutter. These are *his* two and a half minutes, not yours. You are working for him.
- Be flexible because there may be times when you need to take over another helper's position if he is either trying to control a cow or not doing his job.
- Whenever you are helping someone, don't allow your horse to "turn tail" (turn away) to the cow being worked. You must be able to watch what is happening at all times.
- Overhelping can be just as harmful to a cutter's performance as not helping enough. You must know when to step in and move a cow to keep her challenging a horse as well as when to stay away and do almost nothing.
- If you don't feel mentally drained after helping someone, then you probably haven't done your job well.

The Settler

A herd settler, as the term implies, settles a group of cattle before competition begins. He makes sure that the cows are brought into the arena quietly and that they are calm and feeling safe by the back fence. He also lets the herd become comfortable with the center of the arena, and teaches them a pattern of returning slowly to the back fence. How well the settler does his job is important to every rider who works in that particular herd of cattle.

Herd settlers are chosen by the management in larger competitions to assure consistency in the settling process throughout the entire show. In smaller cuttings, the settler is chosen by the first competitor in each herd of cattle. Most often, this settler also participates as a helper for the first competitor.

If you are asked to settle a herd, find out who the other helpers are and ask two or three of them to help you control the cattle when they are brought into the arena. Stand a good distance from the cattle while they enter the pen so that the herd can look around without feeling any pressure. Most cuttings have a holding pen for cattle just behind the center of the back fence, with a gate that leads into the arena. As long as extra cattle are in that pen, the herd will gravitate toward the fence on its own. Otherwise, you should slowly move them with your horse to the center of that fence. Then begins the job of settling the herd so that they feel safe and will stay in one area, regardless of what happens out in front of them.

> If cattle are brought into an arena through a gate that is off to one side of the back fence, they will often want to return to that point instead of settling in the center. In this case, ask a helper to stand near that gate to discourage the cattle from settling there.

Walk your horse back and forth in front of the herd, keeping enough distance so that they don't become upset or scatter. When turning on either side of them, turn *toward* them so that you can keep an eye on any cows that might want to run and take the others along. As soon as the cattle begin to stay closer together at the fence, walk your colt around to one side and get behind them so that you can slowly drive the entire herd toward the center of the arena. Get them familiar with your horse and with being driven to the middle so that they will not panic when the first cutter brings them out.

Survey these cattle while standing behind them. If two or three want to go back to fence, let them, just as long as they move slowly. If one happens to leave at a run, stop her quickly and bring her back to her buddies out in the center. A cow such as this will teach the good cows to run right along with her.

When the cattle are standing quietly in the middle of the pen, ask one of your helpers to step slowly toward them and encourage the herd to return to the back fence. Ideally they should split and move single file around either side of your horse. Whatever path they take, be sure not to block their return, and don't let the leaders come around you too fast—simply make them pause by making one sideways step. Show them that they can move around you as long as they move slowly.

Once the cattle are regrouped at the back fence, walk around to their left or right and bring half of them out by slicing through the herd at an angle. Let these cows return to the fence only by way of the middle portion of the arena, not by going over to either side. Block the ones that want to run. Make a mental note of the cows that "honor" your horse without getting upset, because they will probably be good ones to cut. Then walk around to their other side and again cut through them diagonally, bringing half of the cattle out to the middle.

Entering the herd twice from either side should be sufficient, although cattle will sometimes take more time to establish a suitable pattern of moving. Settle them just long enough that they learn to return to the center of the back fence and stay there. If they are oversettled, they will become bored and lifeless for the competition.

When the cattle will stand at the back fence, trot your horse back and forth in front of them, this time turning away from the herd each time you pass in front so that they'll see the horse's swinging tail. If one cow should break away, just bring her back to the others. Then lope your horse back and forth in front of them a few times. Let the management know when you feel that the cattle are settled, and move into your position as herd holder or turnback helper.

Herd Holders

The two herd holders stand on either side of the herd of cattle near the back fence. Their basic job is to keep the cattle centered and under control there while the cutter is working. When asked by a cutter to "hold herd," this is what you are expected to do:

- Prior to the work, be available to talk with the cutter.
- Help the settler while he settles the cattle.
- Make sure the cattle are centered and quiet at the back fence from the time the cutter enters the arena until the time that his work is over.
- Help the cutter "shape" his cattle.
- Keep the separated cows in the center of the arena while the cutter steps up to make his cut, and then quickly move all other cows back to the herd without interfering with the cutter's work.

- Remain constantly aware of what the herd is doing, making sure that they remain under control and centered on the back fence. At the same time, the herd holder must be aware of what is happening with the cutter and the cow being worked.

Before the Work

When you are asked to help hold the herd, find out if there is something in particular that the cutter wants you to do. He may have a certain cow in mind to cut, or perhaps he wants you to prevent one cow from coming out with the others. He might also tell you how he plans to enter the herd and what his strategy is. Whatever he asks, respect his wishes.

When the cattle are brought into the arena, discourage them from wandering out too far from the back fence by standing near the opposite end of the arena. From this vantage point, you and the cutter, along with his other helpers, can look over the cattle and note any defects (bad eyes, a limp, unhealthy appearance). Stay in the arena until the cattle are settled and it is time for the class to begin.

> Some cutters talk often with their helpers before their "go," whereas others will concentrate solely upon their nerves, their horse, or the cattle they want. As a helper, offer advice only if it is sought.

Entering the Herd

You and the other herd holder will walk your horses toward the herd and quietly center the cattle at the back fence. This is one last opportunity to look them over. You might spot something you missed earlier or see a cow that is breathing hard from being worked. If you see something noteworthy, try to move this cow to the back fence and quietly notify the cutter just as he begins to enter the herd. Then, position your horse so that he is standing fairly near the corner and facing out at an angle between the herd and the center of the arena. From this vantage point you can keep an eye on the cow being worked while also keeping the herd settled at the back fence.

Cattle that have been worked before (called "reruns") will not want to come out. Bunch them together with the other herd holder so that very few are able to hug the back fence.

How close to the corner you should stand when the cutter works will depend upon the cattle. You need to be in a position where you can control cattle should they want to run out, but you must not get in the way of the cutter when he is working as well.

Bringing the Cattle Out

Once the cutter moves behind a few head of cattle and begins to separate those he wants to bring out, work with him to push them toward the middle of the pen. Although he may need very little assistance, you should be ready to step in and help him if the cattle are wild or otherwise difficult to control. This is where you must be able to read cattle. A cutter is hiring you for your judgment, and it is unlikely that he will want to spend any time giving you directions about what to do and how much to do it.

While the cutter is driving the cattle forward, help him control their pace and direction so that he can set them up to make a centered cut. You must simultaneously watch both the cutter and the cows. If the cutter starts to step around a cow he doesn't like, push that cow back to the main herd. The cutter may have indicated that he wants to try to cut a certain cow, in which case you can help to shape that cow toward the front. Follow the cutter's lead. Watch what he's trying to do, then help him without being in the way.

The Cut

As the cows move closer to the center of the arena, you should become very aware of the cutter and of your position on the cows. It is a cutter's responsibility to step up and make his cut, but as a herd holder you can influence the way the cattle begin moving so that his job is easier. If, for example, five head are loosely grouped in the center of the arena, you can encourage one of them to think about moving toward the back fence simply by taking one step toward her hip (or shoulder, depending upon the direction you want her to take). Be subtle here, because she may take off at a dead run, in which case you'd need to block her. Once the cow begins to move, the others will very likely follow, and the cutter can begin to set up the one that he wants to work.

As a herd holder, you can also have a negative influence on cattle while the cutter is trying to step toward them to make his cut. If you trap the cattle out in the center and prevent them from seeing any possibility of returning to the herd at the fence, they are likely to panic and run in all directions. Not only is this situation difficult for a cutter to handle, but it doesn't look good to a judge. The cutter is trying to receive credit for having full control over the cattle and making a "standing cut" in the middle of the arena. He cannot do this if his herd holders are insensitive to the "feel" of those cattle.

Stay with the cutter until there is only *one* cow left in front of him. Work as a team if he has a problem separating the cattle, and then push the other cattle back to the herd as quickly as possible. You should then move toward a corner and into position where you can prevent any cattle from popping out during the cutter's work.

The Work

Your toughest job as herd holder is to contain the herd behind the cutter when cattle are fresh or wild. Even if they appear to be settled near the center of the fence, they can pop out and ruin a cutter's work within seconds. Be ready for such a move. Watch the herd. Read and react to their moves, while at the same time watching the cow that's being worked (*not* the cutter) so you can block her if she comes toward your corner.

It is the cutter's fault if a cow reaches one of the corners of the back fence—he was behind the cow and late. Regardless of fault, try your best not to let that cow return to the herd. Move backwards or sideways to turn the cow away so that the cutter can quit working.

Don't focus entirely on what the cutter is doing, because you'll likely miss something going on in the herd. Focus primarily on the cow being worked as well as the herd at the fence.

Returning to the Herd

When the cutter quits working a cow, step up and move the cow back to the herd out of his way. Then watch the cutter. Help him if he wants to scoop another cow from the front of the herd. Or, if he has trouble getting the cows to come away from the back fence, give him a hand: Bunch them up by crowding them, and force a few out. But never make the cutter's decisions for him, and *never* cut a cow for him: That would detract from the judge's overall impression of what is happening. If the cutter is unable to do a good job and relies heavily on you for help, you should still make every effort to hide that fact. Let the judge think it is the cutter who is in charge.

Turnback Help

The two other helpers stay beyond the area where the cutter works, moving laterally to turn the cow back toward him. Called turnback men, these riders must concentrate as intensely as the cutter does. They should be able to read cattle and should know the difference between *stopping* a cow and *turning* her. Turnback men do not run back and forth with a cow, but they must constantly be in a position to turn her quickly and keep her out in front of the cutter. They may work the entire time or not at all, depending on the cutter's performance and the cows he chooses.

When a cutter asks you to turn back for him, he expects you to do the following:

- Respect his wishes and do your best to help him show his horse to the fullest.
- "Read" each cow that he is working so that you know what is required of you.
- Manipulate the cow's direction when needed, deterring her from going to the side of the pen or out toward the judge's stand.
- Be in a position where you are no more than a few steps away from being able to help the cutter.
- Avoid chasing a cow or forcing her to change direction; *stop* her and let her go back toward the cutter on her own.
- Keep the cow moving so that the cutter's horse stays busy. Lindy Burch says, "The hardest thing for a horse to do is to stay hooked when nothing's happening."
- Avoid making any decisions for the cutter, even though you may feel he should quit working a particularly bad cow or work longer on a good one.
- Know the difference between overhelping and not helping enough, and act only when you believe you will not cause the cutter to lose his working advantage over a cow.

Bringing Them Out

A turnback helper often is not involved with bringing out the cattle. Instead, you will stand farther up the arena when the cattle are brought out in order to prevent them from moving out too far. If, however, one of the herd holders either fails to move out with the cutter or must go back to control the cows at the fence, move in and take his place helping to bring out the cattle.

The Cut

Stay back and remain quiet while the cutter steps up to separate a cow or until the herd holders begin rolling the cattle back toward the cutter. If the cattle are sticky or sour, back up to allow the cutter more room: He will need to bring these cattle out farther in his attempts to separate one.

The Work

Your job begins as soon as a cut has been made and only one cow is left in front of the cutter. If this cow refuses to move, step toward her just enough to get her started. Then work in a lateral fashion to help contain the cow in the center of the arena. Your full concentration is necessary to keep the cutter's horse in balance with the cow. Not only must you be aware of the cutter and his horse, but you need to constantly monitor the horse's position on the cow and your own position in the pen.

Your ability to read cattle is important. Do whatever you think needs to be done to help the cutter, but also be aware that you can make or break a run depending on how you handle each cow:

- You can just as easily "blow the mind" of a good cow as a wild one by overworking her.
- Whenever a cow goes to the fence, she should be slowing down. Any pressure from you can cause her to panic.
- To cope with a "fence-to-fence" cow (one that has a pattern of running from side to side), see whether a quick turn will deter her from heading for the side. Avoid coming in *toward* her when you turn, however, as you may force her to panic and head straight for the cutter. If your quick turn did not help and the cow is running toward the fence at 90 miles per hour, you shouldn't run with her. Instead, stop your horse to take the pressure off the cow, then move back a few steps so that the cutter can quit when the cow turns away from him. But watch the cutter carefully: Should he choose not to quit working this cow, you'll need to be ready to continue helping.
- Credit is given to a cutter who cuts and works a cow in the center of the pen. If the cutter loses this position and moves toward the side, position your horse in a place that will influence the cow to move back toward the center.
- Since a blinded or injured cow will not work well, get out of the way so that the cutter can quit as soon as possible.
- When the cutter has chosen a wild cow, stay back to avoid putting any pressure on her. This type of cow will sometimes calm down after a few turns and begin to work quite well. If the cutter cannot wear her down, he may say that he "wants off," or he may look as though he is having a tough time. Help him get off the cow by giving her space to turn away so that he can quit legally. But *always read the cutter.* He might be trying to put together a winning run on this wild bovine. If that is the case, you need to keep helping.

You can also help when the cutter tells you about a particular problem that he is having with his horse. If he says his colt is easily frightened and needs to build confidence, put no pressure on the cow being worked. With a horse that has a tendency to leak, or roll outward and make barrel turns instead of turning over his hocks, you can help by pushing the cow straight back toward him the moment a cut has been made. This move will surprise a horse and make him begin his work in a defensive manner. Then roll the cow *in* toward the cutter each time she turns by stepping toward her shoulder.

Quitting

Turnback men must be constantly aware of the whole picture and of what the cutter wants. In certain situations, you should act immediately to help the cutter quit and avoid penalty points.

Should a cow pop out from the herd during the work and you are unable to move her quickly out of the way (either behind you or back to their herd), turn the cow being worked *away* so that the cutter can quit legally.

If the cutter picks up slightly on his reins, he is signaling his horse, the judge, and you that he is finished working a cow. If you miss this signal and continue to push the cow in toward him, you might force the cutter to make a "hot quit" and receive penalty points. According to NCHA rules the cutter can quit working a cow only when she is standing still, turned away from him, or is behind the turnback men. If a hot quit happens, don't show any expression. You're there to help your fellow cutter win, not to point out mistakes to the judge.

Armed with the knowledge of each helper's job, you are now capable of choosing good people to help you, and of understanding what they are doing and why they are doing it. You are also prepared to help a fellow competitor should you be asked.

12

PREPARATION

FOR

A SHOW

If you have ever had the pleasure of watching a colt grow to become a cutting horse, or have been atop this athletic and keenly intelligent animal while he is working a cow, you will most likely succumb to the challenge of riding in competition. After all, competition is the way to see how your horse measures up against others of similar age and ability.

Competition can be most rewarding if approached positively. But it will defeat you (and cost a lot of money) if you are not prepared, if your horse is not of the caliber you thought he was, or if you bring along any negative "baggage." There's a great deal to be said for being a "cutter" and participating in cutting events, whether the shows are held in dusty little arenas out in the middle of nowhere or in some of the biggest coliseums in the country. Just approach competition with open eyes. Know what it is you're getting into, and know your own capabilities as well as those of your horse.

Where Do You Fit In?

Your first priority is to learn all you can about competition so that you will have a realistic idea of where you can fit in. Do so early in your training so that you can begin working toward certain goals.

- Contact your regional cutting organization for a schedule of nearby events, and attend a few cuttings as an observer. Local cuttings usually offer classes to include every type of rider, from children to seniors, and from beginners to professionals. There are also classes open to horses of different ability levels, with entry requirements based on a horse's total recorded earnings.
- Join the NCHA to receive a current *Rule Book* and *Casebook*. These manuals explain everything you need to know about the rules of cutting competition and eligibility requirements for each class. You will also receive the *Chatter* magazine, in which you will find information about upcoming events, past ones, and cutting-related topics.
- Study cutting videos that are available for purchase through the *Chatter* or through tack supply stores. Watch how the world's best riders and horses compete in the top money events, you can learn a good deal from them. Pro Barbara Schulte's videos are especially good.
- Get some experience under your belt. Although you must be realistic about your ability (and that of your horse), find a few cuttings in your area to enter as soon as you feel ready. Although not every cutting contest is expensive, most of the NCHA-approved classes have entry fees in the 50- to 500-dollar range. If you are just starting out and want to keep to a low budget, go only to smaller, local shows or to cuttings that are open only to special breeds such as quarter horses, Arabians, Appaloosas, or paints. Both types are low-key, a lot fun, and a good way to learn more about yourself and your horse.
- Limited Age Events, or competitions that are open only to horses between the ages of three and six years, are usually quite large due to the substantial winners' purses. These events have classes for each age of horse, with divisions for professionals, nonpros, beginning nonpro riders, and, often, ladies. Advance planning is a necessity for Aged Event shows because of their size and popularity; you must register and begin paying

part of your entry fees at least four or five months ahead of time. Although your expenses will be greater, these cuttings can be just as much fun as local competitions because of the young and fairly inexperienced horses— budding athletes are not always predictable. The preparation time for horse and rider is much the same for either type of cutting.

Laying the Foundation

Once you have a better idea of what to expect in competition and where you will fit in, spend some time thinking about yourself. Your mind plays a critical role in performance. It takes the same amount of time and effort to groom your psyche and build confidence in yourself as it does to take your horse through the various phases of training. Start early to build a good foundation.

To be a successful showman you must believe in yourself and in your horse. This positive attitude doesn't come easily. It requires many hours in the saddle learning the fundamentals of horsemanship and working on the technical aspects of moving correctly. It means getting to know the ways of cattle. It means recognizing your horse's strengths and weaknesses, his aptitude for cutting a cow and holding her away from the herd. And it means a real *dedication and desire* to continue learning.

At almost every cutting event you will see the top riders there from morning till night, day after day. They spend a lot of time figuring out ways to improve by watching others, studying cattle, and trading ideas. They are students of the sport, going about their business in a positive manner, looking for positive results. A good example is Bill Riddle, who won the 1987 Gold and Silver Stakes in Oklahoma and took home a 1-million-dollar purse. He is said to be one of the greatest students of cutting, spending his time figuring out every cow in a herd before he even walks into an arena.

Preparation

Training becomes serious once you decide to "go down the road." It doesn't matter whether that road leads to the county line or to the national competitions. If you have the foundation and feel that your horse really has the potential to be what Buster Welch calls a "contest horse," then go for it. But be realistic. Don't jump in over your head. First, get to the point where your reactions are automatic, where you can trust your instincts and no longer have to think as hard about when to help your horse and when to let things flow.

Preparing for competition is just like doing homework in school. If you pile on a lot of work at the last minute and try to cram too much into a short amount of time, the chances of success take a real dive. Fear sneaks in the back door, bringing along negative energy that will undermine your performance. This is the time to tune up your horse and tune out everything else. Get tough: use as many different kinds of cattle as you can, and work in different areas so that you know you can handle most situations. Then sharpen up your reactions, focus on correctness, and let yourself get excited about competing.

Before a Show

Readying for competition often will begin several weeks or months before the event, although getting organized to enter local, one-day club competitions is not as complex as preparing for the bigger shows. Most of the classes in smaller cuttings do not offer substantial purse money for the winner, and there are fewer entries (five to twenty per class is average) as a result. You can literally load your horse in a trailer, drive to your destination, register and pay for each class, compete, and go home the same day. Weekend shows are much the same, only with more entries and often bigger purses for some of the classes. Arrangements for a motel and a stall should be made in advance for these two-day competitions.

A larger show, averaging anywhere from thirty to two hundred entries per class, requires more careful planning. You often need to enter classes, reserve stalls, and make hotel reservations several weeks or months ahead of time (each show schedule includes its requirements in an information pamphlet). These shows can last as long as one or two weeks, in which case you'll want to make arrangements for being away from home and work, for the correct amount of bedding and feed, and for your truck and trailer to be serviced.

Plan for each show so that you are adequately prepared in advance and ready to focus on your job instead of worrying about difficulties that could have been avoided. A few examples: You did not allow enough time to correct a certain problem you were having with your horse; your truck broke down because you forgot to change the spark plugs; you forgot to make a stall reservation and there is no space for you; the buckle on your favorite head-stall was broken when you found it in the trailer; you didn't figure out ahead of time when your class started and were unable to warm up your horse adequately. Being upset about *anything*, no matter how small, can undermine your performance.

The Final Week
Before a Show

This final week should be fairly routine. You'll want to work your colt normally, concentrating on his weaker areas, and sharpen his reactions by tuning him several times to get him thinking and respecting you (see chapter 10 on tuning). If he has a problem you can't seem to fix, such as losing concentration when moving to the left, or coming out toward the cow instead of staying back, then it's better not to compete. Bad habits have a way of reappearing during competition.

Other details need to be taken care of during the last few days before a cutting. Check your truck and trailer to make sure everything works: engine, lights, oil, springs, wheel bearings, spare tire, and jack. Call ahead to confirm reservations for a motel and stalls (these preparations should have been done months in advance, along with paying the entry fee, if the competition has a lot of entries). Get *good* directions to the showgrounds from the show secretary. Many cuttings are held at small, out-of-the-way ranches, and there's nothing more frustrating than to wander around the countryside looking for a cutting. Figure out how long it will take to get there and to prepare your horse for the classes. Finally, if a pro or friend will be at the show to help you, find out where to meet and at what time.

The Day Before a Show

The day before a competition, regardless of its size, is a good time to relax mentally and busy yourself with chores. Trim up your horse so that he looks in top shape. Clip his jaw and muzzle, the throat area, his eyelashes, bridlepath, ears, fetlocks, and coronary band. Then lather him up with a good horse shampoo. The addition of a conditioner on his mane and tail will make his hair soft and glossy-looking. Tie him up until he's dry so he doesn't decorate himself with dirt and shavings. You can also braid your horse's tail, fasten it with a rubber band, and leave it in until just before showtime. This keeps it clean and gives it a fuller, wavy look. (Many riders braid a horse's tail or tie it up in a knot every day so that he doesn't step on it when he's working cattle.)

Check over your tack to make sure that everything fits properly and is in good condition. Use a leather conditioner to clean the smooth areas of the saddle and headstall. Then organize and load these items in your trailer:

Shampoo	Absorbine
Fly repellent	Extra halter
Rubber bands for tail	Blankets: summer or winter
Brushes (tail and coat)	Feed and supplement
Hoof pick	Shovel
Salt block	Manure fork
Medicines	Leg wraps
Buckets	Wheelbarrow

Extra items that you may want to include, especially if you have a long trip ahead or if you are transporting mares or studs:

- Vicks VapoRub (to put on a stud's nose so he can't smell and be distracted by mares in heat)
- Piece of copper wire (some say that putting a piece in a mare's water helps curb the estrous cycle)
- Electrolyte powder from a vet supply store, or Gatorade from the market (to help replenish fluid loss and restore muscle energy during hot weather)
- Karo syrup (to sweeten water in case your horse doesn't like the local variety)
- Shipping boots (always a good idea when on the road because they protect the entire lower leg and coronary band)
- Leg wraps (wrapping a horse's legs, especially in winter, helps prevent swelling)
- Baking soda (one tablespoon in each feeding can help prevent colic and "grassy stomach" when a horse is nervous and not eating as he normally would)

Wood shavings or straw on top of the rubber mats in your trailer help protect a horse's legs from road heat on a long trip. Its presence also encourages him to urinate normally (studs and geldings don't like to urinate in a trailer, especially when it's moving).

Most people feed their horses in transit. If you have feed nets or mangers, you can keep your horse tied to the trailer while he eats during the trip.

Otherwise, if you feel your horse will be secure, put the hay on the floor and unhook the lead rope. However, it's never a good idea to unhook a stud's lead rope.

Traveling

Allow plenty of time to get to your destination, find a parking place, register, and warm up. Taking the "hurry" out of travel is another way to curb anxieties that can undermine a positive attitude.

Driving a loaded horse trailer takes some practice. Sharp turns or stops will tire a horse out and can injure him. If your trip is longer than five or six hours, stop for a short time to check the horses and let them relax from the vibration. Have them arrive as fresh and alert as possible.

Timing Your Arrival

Regardless of what time their classes begin, most competitors will spend all day at a cutting. However, you may have other obligations and not want to arrive earlier or stay later than necessary. Here are a few ways to plan your timing more carefully so as to arrive in time to register, get ready, warm up, and compete:

- *Smaller (one- or two-day) cuttings.* A schedule of events is usually published and mailed to you ahead of time. If not, call the show secretary, whose name is available at your regional club or published in the *Chatter* (true for every NCHA-sponsored event). Find out what time competition begins, the number of classes prior to yours, and the approximate number of entries in those classes (this is not always available since registration often occurs on the day of the show). As a rule of thumb, each "go" takes a total of five minutes; a class with ten riders will take approximately one hour, including time to settle the cattle. Finally, you must register for your class a *minimum* of one class prior to it.
- *Larger cuttings.* Although registration, payment, and stall reservations are done ahead of time, you will need adequate time to find the office, the secretary, your assigned stall, bedding for the stall, a parking spot nearby, the sign-up sheet for practice works, and a list showing your draw. This takes *a lot* of time (an hour or two at least) simply because of the number of competitors and horses at a larger show.

Arrival

Park where you have enough room to tie your horse safely to the trailer without being in anyone's way. If the area around you happens to be clean and neat, respect it (don't shovel manure and shavings out the back door of your trailer). Then take care of your horse. Put him in his stall, if appropriate, or tie him to the trailer and give him water.

Showgrounds are almost always open at least one hour prior to the start of a show. If you arrive early, groom and saddle up so that you can ride around in the arena before the show starts. This is a good way to learn about the pen and to get your horse accustomed to the new surroundings. If you have brought a two-year-old along, tie him up somewhere in the arena so that he can look around and get used to things. Then figure out how much time there will be before your class so that you can adjust your warm-up accordingly.

If you are a newcomer, ask a trainer or friend to help you prepare for your class. Although you should be the one to warm up your horse and to get the feel of him on the day of a show, your trainer might want to sharpen him up and get him thinking just before you compete. He can also give you some advice about your riding technique or about strategy: there may be reasons to enter the herd from a certain side, to stay away from a particular cow, or to ride in a certain way.

Don't be embarrassed to ask for help. Many accomplished riders, even pros who are friends, bounce ideas off of each other before and after they compete. This is what makes the sport of cutting unique. Almost every rider is willing to help another when needed, regardless of the fact that they are competitors. You'll find this especially true of smaller cuttings where most people know each other and where the purse money is not high.

13

WARMING UP

The transition from home turf to a show situation can make the warming-up process fairly tricky, especially when you have a young colt or a horse that tends to be nervous. Try to calculate the time it will take to prepare your horse so he is ready to give 100 percent of his effort toward working a cow. He needs to be relaxed and loose, with enough energy to do his job well. And he should "feel" right to you.

Planning Ahead

In order to plan your warm-up, figure out the approximate time you will compete and decide whether you want first to tune up your horse in the practice pen. Find out the order of classes and how many people are before you. Allow two or three hours before your "go" to prepare yourself and your horse. If you "draw up" first in one class at a small cutting, it's your responsibility to arrange for the herd to be settled by one of your helpers and to be warmed up and ready to compete. The bigger cuttings usually have prechosen herd settlers, and a draw that is published prior to the show. In this case, it takes only a little bit of calculating to estimate the time you will be showing.

Bigger cuttings often have practice pens that are open to riders wishing to tune up their horses or colts on "used" cattle. There is a charge for practice, and a time limit of about five minutes. If you want to tune your horse, plan to sign up early so that you can practice and then let him relax before competing. The person in charge of this pen is always available and can help you plan your time correctly.

The Warm-up Area

Be prepared for anything when it comes to the type of space reserved for warming up at a show. Areas vary greatly in size and footing, and they are guaranteed to be crowded with riders. Don't become upset about a less-than-ideal situation; simply adjust to it, formulate a plan, and focus on your job. If the pen happens to be small and crammed with riders who seem to be socializing instead of working, warm up your horse early in the day when no one is around. If the footing is rock hard (in some cases it may even be asphalt), warm up by walking your horse in small circles for a few minutes. Find out the limitations, then work within them.

Warming Up

The warm-up will depend upon your horse and how he feels that day. Listen to him and find out what he needs. You'll need to relax him if he's nervous.

This might mean a lot of loping, or it could require walking in big, easy circles. If he's feeling normal, then warm up exactly as you would at home: Long-trot, lope in big circles while tipping his head and neck slightly to the outside, move him forward and backward in a straight line, and stop and turn him around. Your goal is to take the edge off without exhausting or scaring him or teaching him anything new (schooling should have been done at home).

Some people will lope a horse for two or three hours and then just sit on him until their class begins. It's better to dismount, loosen the cinch, and let a horse relax. You can ride him around again to wake him up a few minutes before your turn. Also, be considerate of others who are warming up with you. Roaring around a small area and upsetting other riders and horses is not very thoughtful.

Certain horses are more easily distracted or high-strung than others. If you are going to show a younger horse in Aged Events, a mare "in season," or a stud, warm them up and have them ready early. Be sure to allow enough time before your class (at least an hour or two) for a good, long warm-up: Your colt will need to be fairly tired so that he's not distracted from his work.

The subject of warming up at a show is often brought up during clinics. The following examples may be useful:

- Lindy Burch spends a good deal of time long-trotting her colts because it's their most natural gait. A horse will reach out and stay low to the ground as he moves forward, and this is good preparation for working a cow.
- Chubby Turner feels that some horses will trick you into thinking they're warmed up. His technique for deciding whether a horse is ready to work is to ask him to go faster. If he speeds up for more than a few strides, then he's not warmed up enough.
- Mike Haack warms up his young colts early, then ties them somewhere in the arena so they can have a good long look at everything for an hour or two. Then, just before the class, he'll ride again for a few minutes to loosen them up.

Hiring Help

Lindy Burch says, "When you hire help, you hire their judgment. Choose people who can read cattle and read what you want them to do."

Before your class, figure out whom you want to use as helpers. If you are new to cutting and don't know anyone, watch the riders who are helping others. Try to determine whether they are doing their job and seem interested. Wait until they are in the warm-up area and then introduce yourself. If you are working with a pro, he will be planning to help you and can suggest others who would be good.

When asking someone to help, make sure he has the time and energy to be there 100 percent. Some riders are asked to help constantly and may need a break. Also, most of these people bring their own horses and use them all day long. Horses need a break, too. So be considerate. Besides, when they're tired, they might not do as good a job for you.

How many times have you heard a cutter ask helpers who are already inside the arena, "Jack, will you stay where you are? And Barb, can you sit in the corner? I'm up *right now*." Or, "Will everyone just stay where they are?" These people are not going to walk out and refuse to help when you've trapped them into it, but they may be less than enthusiastic to do their very best. Ask them for their help ahead of time. Give them an opportunity to answer you honestly.

Let your helpers know what you want to try to do in the arena. Maybe you want to work a certain cow, or perhaps your horse needs a cow pushed right toward him to make that first turn an explosive one. This is *your* time. If you want to split the herd down the middle, then let your helpers know. If you want some pointers, then ask. But don't let them intimidate you if you're not as good a rider or have less experience than they. They're there to help you try to win, even though, ultimately, winning is up to you.

When you've done all you can do, sit back and focus on showing your horse to that judge. Don't push away the little twinges of anxiety that start to creep in. Instead, get your head in gear and make those nerves work *for* you.

I rode in my first futurity on a colt that I had purchased from David Holmes in Oregon. He watched me as I began to fret about the other riders in my class. I felt like the underdog having to compete against highly experienced riders, including the wives of top pros. David's way of looking at this was the key to my success that year. He told me that I couldn't change the system and that, instead, I had to figure out a way to go in there and beat my competition.

Go to a cutting prepared to show your horse to his best advantage, and you will get something out of it. Be positive when you prepare your horse in the warm-up pen, and it will carry you through competition.

14

THE

COMPETITION

You win at cuttings by adapting to the situation better than others do.

–CHUBBY TURNER

Watching the Cattle

Whether you are first up or last in the bunch, be present when your herd of cattle comes into the pen to be settled so that you can clearly see each cow and begin to formulate a plan for your run. In most competitions, you can stand quietly just inside the cutting pen to watch (the bigger shows, however, often allow only the first contestant and his helpers to be in the working arena).

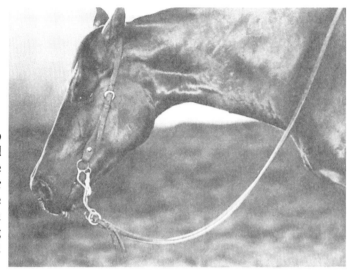

A horse that is ready to enter the arena is warmed up and relaxed, yet he knows that his rider means business. The reins are loose and even so that the bit can hang properly in his mouth while he works a cow.

Note the behavior patterns of the herd and get a good reading on each cow as she moves around the settler's horse. Cattle are a lot like homing pigeons: They tend to move as a group, and they will either return to the gate through which they entered or move to where they can be near other cattle. The direction they naturally want to take will be evident as the settler moves behind them to bring them out. Their pattern can affect the way you choose to enter the herd. If, for example, their natural flow is clockwise, you might want to enter from the right so that you can slow or stop the pattern they have developed. This can give you more time to get set up behind them before bringing them away from the back fence.

Make a mental note of the cattle that look unhealthy, lost, wild-eyed, or high-headed: They are not likely to be good cutting prospects. Remember them as you would at home by features that you can recognize again from horseback, such as their coloring, the tops of their heads, their ears, their backs, and tails.

Settling is also a good time to be thinking about your draw and how it will affect the cattle you choose. If you are one of the first to go, the cows that "want" to be cut will be more content to walk out when the settler brings them toward the center of the arena, while the bad ones are going to move back to the fence. These cattle are likely to react the same way when you walk into the herd, and your job of setting up the good ones to cut should not be difficult. Being placed later in the draw requires more attention on your part: Not only must you think about the cattle while they are being settled, but you should watch them during each work prior to yours. Note the bad ones and those that have been overworked by another cutter, check to see whether the ones you liked have been cut, and watch the way each rider approaches the herd and how the cattle respond. If every rider enters from the left side, you can disrupt their flow and possibly flush out a good cow by entering from a different direction.

Preparation

Because settling may take anywhere from ten to thirty minutes, walk your horse around to keep him loosened up. If you are first, take care of any last-minute details ahead of time (chaps and hat secure, hooves picked, splint boots on, and cinch adjusted) so that you can concentrate solely on your horse. He may be warmed up and ready, but he can lose some of his intensity while you are watching the herd or waiting to go. To raise his level of concentration again a few minutes before you go, back him up straight, turn him around in each direction, and then back up again. Quicken him up. Get him thinking about his job, but take care not to scare him at this time: His mind must be focused on the cow when he walks into the arena.

When you are next to go, wait in the area just behind the judges' stand where you can see the cattle. Mentally rehearse your run by imagining it's you who is out there working that cow, picturing each stop being rock solid and perfect. Read the cow's every move to get your timing exact. Then, discuss any last-minute plans with your help: How you will enter the herd, what you want to try to do, and whether there are certain cows that you wish to avoid or to shape toward the front. If the cattle are bad, ask your help to try to pick the best ones and bunch them together so that they are easier to bring out. If your horse has a particular problem (such as leaking out or being long on one side), tell your helpers so that they can try to avoid exposing those weaknesses.

While your helpers move into position, run through last-minute checks: your hat snug, your reins even and slackened to the length you want (some riders feed out more rein later when making a cut). Then back up your horse one more time, take a deep breath, and relax. The fun's ahead.

Approaching the Herd

As soon as your helpers have the cattle centered and ready, walk quietly toward the herd at the angle you've chosen, and begin to focus on your job. Think *only* about the first goal: entering the herd quietly and with little disturbance to the cattle.

Trainer and showwoman Lindy Burch approaches the herd at an angle. She is physically relaxed, but mentally alert. As she urges her horse slowly forward, she is planning how to manipulate and shape the cattle she wants to bring to the front.

Pro Chubby Turner steps toward a few cattle while letting those on his right return to the herd. He has a look of confidence and control. Although he has not yet "committed" to the cow he wants to cut, Turner is sorting through the possibilities and letting two of them return to the herd while he steps farther forward.

Every cutter has his own way of dealing with nerves as he walks toward the herd. He may shift in the saddle, cough, scratch his nose, wipe his eyes, wiggle his toes, or adjust his hat for the seventh time. Or he may just sit there, looking serious. Whatever your particular quirk, don't worry about it. Just concentrate on the business ahead.

Slow down as you get closer to the herd so that you can see how they are going to react to you and your horse. If they are fresh, some "volunteers" might wander out toward the center. Those on the wild side will be easily upset by any quick movement. The sour ones will have their tails, instead of their heads, facing you. Find the cattle you want to cut and the ones that spell trouble—know where they are in relation to the others. And keep up a dialogue with your herd holders; talking is not penalized unless you purposely disturb the cattle.

Entering the Herd

Because one deep cut is mandatory in any NCHA-sponsored event, most riders elect to satisfy the requirement when they first enter the herd so that they won't have to worry about doing it later. This is also a good way to survey the cattle at the beginning of a run. But there will be times when it's not wise to make a deep cut at first. If you are first in the group, you might be better off taking the four, five, or six cows standing toward the front of the herd. This way, you can avoid the risk of scattering the others that are still unsure of where to stay. Much time is wasted by a cutter who marches in and scares the cattle. He must then wait for the helpers to get things under control again before a cut can be made.

If you do decide to take only a few head of cattle, be sure that you move in *behind* them to bring them out. Not only will you have better control over them, but you might also satisfy the deep-cut rule.

One cow might wander out toward the middle of the pen just as you begin to enter the herd. If she looks good to you, change your plan of making a deep cut and get your horse set up behind her. Avoid any extra reining, to make it seem like this was your original plan. Let the judge think you are in control here. Work that cow, and then return to the herd to make your deep cut.

Bringing Out the Cattle

Herdwork is not only important,
it's most important.
–CHUBBY TURNER

Wait until your helpers are in position and ready before you bring out cattle. They are there to assist in setting things up so that you can make a good cut. When ready, step slowly toward some of the cows. Then hesitate. You can tell a lot about the cattle by moving cautiously: The bad ones will duck their heads and leave, and the better ones will stay where they are or begin to walk forward. Get behind those cattle that you want to push forward and slowly begin moving them as a group toward the center of the arena. This is when you can start to manipulate the ones you want to cut, to whittle away at the herd until you've set the stage for a good, clean cut.

A common problem with the novice rider is that he tends to hurry this portion of the cut, looking as though he is marching out for battle. He misses good cows because he doesn't calculate his moves to keep them out in front of his horse. He doesn't think about how to *work* a herd. Accomplished nonpro Julie Roddy knows how to receive credit for her excellent herdwork. She has learned to take her time, to get a feel for the cattle, and to study her options before bringing them out. And, as a result, she wins many competitions around the country.

Moving Up the Arena

Treat each cow differently. Recognize where you
have to be on a specific cow to shape
her to where you want her to go.
–BILL FREEMAN

Here is when shaping comes into play. You will quietly be trying to peel away the bad cows while manipulating the ones you want to move to the center of the pen. Chubby Turner calls this "painting a picture for the judge." Let the judge know that you are in control of these cattle and that you have a plan in mind. He or she will give you credit for good herdwork.

Continue to walk behind the cows, zig-zagging slightly to see which ones shape toward the middle and which ones aren't going to cooperate. Keep an eye on the potential leaders (the ones on the outside) and try to keep them under control—if they were to decide to head for the back fence, they would take the good cows along with them.

Zig-zagging behind the cattle is also a way to subtly remind your colt to listen to you and to move off your leg. As long as you are not too obvious about giving him signals with your rein or leg, you will not be penalized by the judge.

If you step aside to let a certain cow escape, your herd holders should be paying close attention. They can help by not blocking her departure. Otherwise, that cow might reenter the group again.

The closer you get to where you want to make your cut, the more you need to avoid tunnel vision. Watch the lead (or point) cow, but don't be so intent on her that you lose sight of the whole picture. If you want to shape her toward the middle where you can make a centered cut (and receive credit for doing so), keep looking around instead of staring at her while you figure out how to get her there. Use the other cattle to manipulate her. This way, you haven't closed off your options entirely should another cow move into a better position to be cut.

Choosing the
Correct Area to Make a Cut

As in practice at home, you need sufficient space between your horse and the herd in order to be able to work and to fade backwards when a tough cow is challenging. In competition, driving cattle far from the herd shows the judge that you can control them (a credit), and it helps to prevent any disturbance to the herd while you are working (a penalty). But be aware of the cattle you are driving forward. Watch how they react to you so that you don't push them too far and cause them to panic:

- If you want to cut a high-headed type (a Brahma or a tiger stripe, for instance), it's better to drive as far as you can so that you have plenty of room to retreat. They are not predictable and can put a lot of pressure on a horse when they decide to return to the herd.
- If you have drawn an early position in your group of cattle, drive out far so that the rest of the herd won't decide to join you while you are working. Ample distance also makes it easier for your herd holders to contain the rest of these fresh cattle at the fence.

- If you have drawn a later position, don't worry as much about the other cattle interrupting your work because they are not likely to leave the safety of the back fence. But be sure to drive out far enough to give yourself a good amount of working space so that the judge will give you credit.

Bill Freeman wins many cuttings because of his excellent herdwork. He often has a big advantage before he is even clear of the herd just because of the way he sets up his cows. He is quiet and calculating, yet assertive. And he maintains that image throughout the entire work.

Setting Up for the Cut

Keep a mental picture of what the "perfect" cut looks like. You've practiced making good cuts at home with many different types of cattle and under all kinds of conditions. It shouldn't be any different now. Get your cow set up in the center so that you can receive credit from the judge, and then keep her there (your herd holders can help) so that all you have to do is drop your rein as soon as the other cattle have begun to move back toward the fence. Being in the center will also help your horse begin working the cow in a balanced manner.

To start the cattle flowing around you, move your horse a step to one side so they can see an opportunity to return to the herd at the fence. When they begin to move, take another step forward and make them hesitate. You might find a cow or two that will stop to "honor" your horse instead of starting to run. These are good ones to cut. If the cattle still don't move, take another step forward. Give them a nudge, then back up so that you are again in a better position to make your cut.

One of your herd holders should be helping to get the cattle moving at this point, but don't depend on it; you should be able to do so by yourself.

When cattle start to "roll," or move as a group around you back toward the fence, don't stand there numbly, giving them the advantage. Keep sneaking toward the shoulder of the cow you want. Be very subtle, though, when stepping toward any one cow. You don't want to commit to working her until you are absolutely certain you can get her separated. If you can control this cow, you may be able to get a "standing cut" where the cow is not moving (credit is given for this). If, however, the last two cows "buddy up," you'll

After having separated a cow, Chubby Turner makes certain that his horse is "hooked" before he drops the reins onto the horse's neck. Although he may have received a penalty point from the judge here, Turner knows that his colt is now completely focused on the cow.

need to separate them before dropping your rein and beginning work. Take a step toward one of them to find out which is less likely to run from you. Then step between them and be ready to go with the cow you want. This difficult situation is one that you should have practiced at home to avoid frustration and hurry. You want to handle it with as much finesse as you can, then focus on the rest of your work.

When I began competing, I relied heavily upon my help to assist me in setting up a cow to cut. I was actually more like a spectator; they did most of the work. But that is not *cutting*. I didn't show the judge that I was in control of the situation, nor did I keep my horse interested. Then I began to watch tapes and study some of the well-known cattlemen work a herd and choose a cow. Buster Welch, Don Dodge, Shorty Freeman, Larry Reeder, Mike Mowry, Leon Harrel, and Pat Patterson are all masters at picking cattle and making a cut. They do not rely upon their helpers to do what they should be doing themselves. They know cattle, and can figure out ways to get out of bad situations and set up good ones. And they can do it alone.

The moment that only one cow is left standing in front of you, and you *know* your horse is hooked and intently watching her, drop your rein onto his neck and squeeze him slightly with your legs to increase his intensity. Let him know he's supposed to get to work.

The Work:
Controlling the Cow

The idea is for us to work the cow,
not the opposite.
–CHUBBY TURNER

The very first move your horse makes must be quick, correct, and assertive if he is to establish control over the cow in front of him. If you feel that he is less than 100 percent certain of his left and right parameters, then establish them *before* you drop your hand onto his neck to let him work. This should be done when you are in the process of driving the cattle forward (zig-zagging behind them while subtly using your leg to move him over, and your rein to check his forward movement), but you may need to remind him more strongly after you've separated a cow. Even though points are subtracted each time you rein your horse after having made a cut, it is important that you get him focused and in control of the cow before turning him loose.

> Chubby Turner said, "A point or two for reining at the beginning of your run will be earned back twofold with a solid and correct performance."

When you began training at home with a herd, you taught your colt how to rate a cow by staying across from her hip or belly. Often this entailed using the entire width of the pen, and your goal was to teach the colt to stay in the correct position with the cow. As he advanced in training, you asked your colt to be more aggressive with a cow in the center portion of the pen. This required that you push him forward into a controlling position across from the cow's neck or head.

Now that you are in competition, not only will you want to show a judge that you can control a cow, but that you can often control her in the center portion of the arena. This requires certain moments where you push the horse farther forward than the cow's neck or head to stop her before she gets close to either side of the fence.

The moment that the cow moves, the horse is centered and balanced, alert and intent only on the cow in front of him.

Knowing when to "shut down" a cow, or stop her in her tracks, requires quick thinking on your part. You have to figure out the exact time to become more aggressive with her. You have to "get inside her mind," as cutters say. If you overreact by constantly trying to move ahead of her, she will very likely outmaneuver your horse and get back to the herd. You will lose almost any chance of winning the competition. Instead, set her up. If you cannot shut her down with a quick, aggressive turn in the center of the pen, then rate her (usually with your horse in position across from her neck) until you can find the right moment to stop her. Again, show the judge that you are in control.

Buster Welch related this setting-up time to a boxing match, when Larry Holmes broke Muhammad Ali's jaw with a "haymaker." This famous punch didn't just happen out of the blue; Holmes used fifty sharp jabs to set Ali up first. It's the same with cutting, Welch said. If a horse jumps out and makes those big haymakers, the cow will break him if she knows what she's doing. But if a horse sets her up by just "pushing the outside of the envelope" instead of losing his advantage, he will be in position to break the cow.

Often we are reluctant to ask a horse to do more than we've been training him to do. But if you are to have a winning run in stiff competition, you must go all out and expose yourself to challenge. You must react instantly to any situation, knowing exactly when to push your horse a little bit harder and when to melt down in the saddle, helping protect him from an impossible situation. If your horse can jump out ahead of a cow, and in the very next move jump to the other side and trap her, he's doing something which has a high degree of difficulty (an "attaboy," as Buster Welch calls it). But he can't do this day after day. You need to be smart about when and when not to ask him for more.

Stopping and Turning

It's a lot harder to change
a cow's mind once she's made it than to
help her make her decision.
–LINDY BURCH

The key to controlling a cow is to control her in the *beginning* of her turn. If you miss here, it's much harder to correct because you are already a step behind the cow. This quick, decisive turn is based on having a good, solid, down-in-the-ground stop. Bill Freeman's descriptive comments about "bottoming out in the stop" and "riding with the seat of your pants" describe what you need to do to get your horse balanced and ready for the full, sweeping turns that add drama to your work. Think *stop* by sitting down deep in your saddle. Help your horse prepare to control that cow. Get your toes out and spurs ready so you can ride through each turn completely and then push down on the gas pedal.

Many different situations will arise during your two-and-a-half minutes of work. Here are typical ones, with suggested responses:

- If you cut a good cow, use him up so that someone else won't come in and beat you on the same cow. This is the kind of cow you can be more aggressive with. Show the judge that she cannot push your horse around.
- If you cut a wild cow, quit as soon as you can so that you don't lose her, or try to wear her down so you can work her in the middle of the pen. Then go find a better cow to make an impression on the judge. You can't score a 74 on a 68 type of cow.
- You will not score a high mark on a cow that refuses to move around. Make a few correct turns to demonstrate you can control her, then

Working a tough cow, Lindy Burch makes a decisive and rapid turn in order to prevent the cow from having the advantage coming out of the turn.

quit. Don't make your horse dance around or turn unnecessarily in front of a cow that is just standing there.

- Dealing with a tough, aggressive "alligator" requires great care and timing. It would be a risk to step out ahead of this type of cow to try to control or stop her, because most likely you'd lose her. Instead, just rate her until you can either wear her down to where she'll begin responding to your horse, or until you can find the right moment to quit.
- You might stop correctly with a cow only to find that she has faked your horse into making a turn. You're in a bad spot when this happens. You can only sit tight, without leaning or giving any other indication that something is wrong. If your horse can hook up again and get back into position, it may save your run. But if you interfere by picking up the reins, you'll lose points.
- Don't become so involved in what the cow is doing that you forget about the herd behind you and how close you are to them. Getting too close to the herd and disturbing them will not only cause a penalty, but is a difficult situation to get out of. You can use your herd-side leg to push the horse out and away from the cattle, but this may cause him to come out too far and set him up to lose the cow. You can also wait for

the cow to turn away from you and then quit. Neither way looks very good to a judge and both can result in a penalty.

• If a cow has pushed you back toward the corner, it means that you were out of position in the first place, trailing her across the pen instead of staying across from her head or shoulder. Should this happen, you'll have to use your herd-side leg to move your horse out toward the cow in order to avoid running into the herd. But, as in the above situation, this might cause him to come out even farther in subsequent turns. Keep the pressure on after every turn so that the cow doesn't get the upper hand.

• Some cows will turn away from your horse or move in a big arc. This can draw your horse out farther and set him up to lose a cow unless you are quick to correct him with your legs and can use body language to slow him down.

Quitting a Cow

With enough practice at home, quitting a cow correctly (when she's obviously turned away or stopped) will come naturally to you. But there are a few things to be aware of when you are in a competitive situation and wish to make the best of every second. Quitting at just the right time creates an impression of confidence and control.

When to quit working a cow is a judgment call of sorts because of all the variables. You must consider the type of cow and the length of time you've worked her. You have to know your horse. And you need to consider how much time is left, because it looks best to be in the process of working a cow when the buzzer signals the end of your two-and-a-half minute run.

Begin looking for the right time and place to quit as soon as the cow loses the *feel* you want, or as soon as your horse begins to lose his intensity. In either case, trust your intuition, and the chances are excellent that you will be able to quit her when you still have the advantage. Read when she is going to stop, and then be quick and decisive about your signal to quit so that both the horse and the judge get your message. Pick up on the reins, and put your other hand on the horse's neck. Then turn back in the direction you would move when working a cow (toward the judge and the center of the pen), and walk to the herd.

Quitting a cow in competition always seems to have its problems. Try to be prepared for anything so that you can respond quickly and decisively.

- If you want to quit working a bad cow (one that is wild or runs from fence to fence), the best you can hope for is that one of your corner helpers will read the situation and step out to push the cow away from you. You then have the opportunity to quit without penalty points. But don't be caught *expecting* a helper to do so; he cannot read your mind, and he might be busy trying to contain the herd at the fence. Also, don't get caught short (and out of position) on a cow by relaxing when you think your corner help is about to save you. Cows can change direction and outmaneuver a horse that is even slightly out of position.
- If a second cow suddenly joins the contest, your helpers may be able to separate the new one quickly and push her out of the way. But if this isn't possible you must either pick up the reins to keep your horse working the correct cow (with penalty points each time you rein him), wait until the cow you were working turns away so that you can quit legally, or have a "hot quit." If your helpers are doing their job they will turn both cows away from you so that you can quit.
- If you decide to quit while at the side of the pen, try to bring the judges' attention back toward the center by turning your horse in that direction. Even though you weren't able to have a perfect quit in the middle of the pen, you can create the illusion of having done so. It may help the judges perceive your quit in a more positive way.

Quitting a cow is a good time to sneak in a little schooling if your horse should need it. You can push your spur into his belly while holding his forward motion and make him turn around. If done subtly, you will catch your horse's attention without risking penalty points. But doing something obvious, such as backing him or making him pivot quickly, is considered to be grounds for a penalty.

Returning to the Herd

Every time you quit working a cow, return to the herd with purpose. Take the shortest route, showing the judge that you are not wasting time. Then, slow down when you get close to the herd. Allow yourself time to look over the other cattle and formulate a plan. But be aware of the time remaining so that you can pace yourself and avoid "dying in the herd" when the buzzer sounds to end your work.

Schooling

"Schooling" not only means training in general, it also means correcting your horse in front of the judges during competition. Every rider is bound to have a problem with his horse at some point, and there will be certain times when it's best to school him then and there instead of waiting until you get home. If he should misbehave, for example, or stop working entirely, or forget to turn with a cow, school him. But this shouldn't happen often because it usually means you are doing something wrong at home. Besides, pulling on the reins or spurring hard more than a couple of times not only looks bad, it ruins the cattle for subsequent competitors by frightening them and wearing them out. Cattle need to be as fresh and responsive as possible for every rider in the class. Correct your horse, if need be, and then let him work again. If he is still unresponsive, stay with the same cow and correct him one more time. Then have the courtesy to stop working, regardless of how much time is left.

When the Buzzer Sounds

When time is called, pick up on the reins and put your free hand on the horse's neck. Again, be definite. Try to find a good time to do it so that you don't pull your horse off the cow just as she's challenging him, but don't work any longer than absolutely necessary—it's not fair to other competitors who may want to use that same cow. Then, leave the arena with the attitude that you did your best and will do even better the next time.

Once outside the arena, dismount, loosen your horse's cinch, and take off his splint boots. Walk him around to cool off, then give him a bath. If you are angry about something he did wrong, don't punish him for it now because he has too short a memory: A horse learns from his mistakes only when you correct him the moment he makes one. It's likely you'll see these mistakes again at home where you can take care of them.

Your education as a rider and showman should continue after you leave the arena. Evaluate your performance while it's fresh in your mind, and be objective about how you did in there. Solicited comments from others, in small doses, can be quite helpful at times. If you have a trainer, talk things over with him. Most cuttings are routinely taped on video. You can review your run immediately or order a tape to study at home. Above all, *be positive*. Too many complainers and blamers can put a damper on everyone's fun. Try to figure out what happened, and why. Then start working on how to improve it. If you didn't do well, there will always be another show—always another cutting down the road.

The Elements of Judging

Today's stringent NCHA rules have made judging more uniform than in the past. Every NCHA judge must attend biannual seminars, satisfactorily pass the Association's tests, officiate at a minimum number of competitions yearly, and answer to the director of judges for every work that he scores. The NCHA also has developed a rating system under which each judge is classified according to his experience and judging record. As a result, today's competitors can show under any NCHA-approved judge in the country and expect to receive approximately the same score for a similar run.

Although a judge's score is subjective, he bases it on a point system of credits and penalties similar to that in skating or diving competitions. He scores a cutter's work between a low of 60 and perfect run of 80 points. An average run is a 70, and a top-scoring run is rarely higher than 75 or 76 (see appendixes A and B for specific credit and penalty points and the NCHA Judge's Card). A score of 0 occurs either when a rider leaves the arena before his time expires or when he uses illegal equipment on his horse. Not always shown by specific marks on the score sheet, but evident when arriving at the final score, is the human element of judging: the way a judge subjectively perceives the content of each run. This delicate human factor often separates two or three runs that otherwise may be comparable.

When you first approach the herd, you have the average score of 70. As your work progresses, this score fluctuates according to the judge's analysis of your run content. He considers the following:

- Your herdwork
- The distance you drive a cow from the herd
- Whether your reins are sufficiently loose during the entire work
- Your ability to set up and then work a cow near the center of the arena
- The degree of difficulty of your run
- The eye appeal of you and your horse
- The overall performance
- The amount of courage you demonstrate
- The amount of time that is spent actually working cattle

Also during your run, the judge will separately note all penalty points. When the buzzer sounds to end your work, he puts a numerical value on your run and then subtracts the penalty points. Your score is the result.

You win a cutting by separating your run from your competitor's, even if it's only by half a point. To do so, you must know the *Rule Book* and know what is needed to impress a judge and increase his evaluation of the run content. Seven NCHA judges have offered their ideas about what adds or detracts from a run (the judges are: Mike Kelly and Rod Edwards from Texas, Joe Jones and Tim Smith from California, Brent Layton from Utah, Todd Williamson from Idaho, and Sam Shepard from Alabama). Here are their comments:

What a Judge Does Not *Like to See*

- Having to think about those close calls because the rider was not definite in his actions
- A rider who obviously waits for the last cow every time instead of showing some initiative in making his cuts. Many judges feel that there is not enough emphasis put on this, especially at the Aged Events.
- A rider who plays it safe and stays out of trouble when working a very good cow. Average runs become monotonous. A judge wants to see a rider *show* his horse. He wants to be excited about what he's watching.
- A rider who is obviously confused and indecisive about which cow to cut and when to quit
- A rider who cuts a good cow and then works it for only three or four turns
- A rider who bails out of a bad situation by simply pulling up and quitting
- "Barrel turns" instead of good, solid turns over the hocks
- A horse that overworks a soft cow by making a lot of unnecessary moves
- Helpers who interfere too much, either by cutting the cow for the rider, stopping a cow, or turning a cow when the cutter's horse cannot do so

What a Judge Likes *to See in a Cutting Horse*

- An athlete—a horse that is built to handle quick moves and hard stops, and can demonstrate his ability to control a tough cow.
- Expression—a horse that *looks* interested in outthinking and outmaneuvering the cow. "I like to see a natural: a real cow horse that is genuinely intent on the cow because of his instincts and his training." (Brent Layton)
- Eye appeal—little subtleties may make a difference, especially at the higher level where riders and horses are harder to separate by score. An example would be a horse that traps a cow while staying low and balanced instead of having to elevate his front end through each turn.

What a Judge
Likes *to See in a Rider*

- A rider who outsmarts and outshows his opponents by demonstrating confidence, courage, and control of each cow he cuts. "Show me what you brought. Show me what this horse can do." (Rod Edwards)
- One who takes some risk in front of the judge: committing early to a cow instead of waiting until one separates itself from the others; working a tough cow just a little longer than may be "safe"; continuing to work a cow until the buzzer sounds instead of quitting and "dying" in the herd.
- A good attitude. A positive rider presents himself and his horse in a professional manner, shows incentive, and does whatever he can to avoid penalties and add credits to his run.
- One who gives the judge a reason to mark him higher than the next person. "A good nonpro is on the offensive. He asks his horse to control the cow whenever possible, striving to get the most he can out of his run." (Mike Kelly)
- "I like a person who shows a horse with his hand down on the horse's neck. A raised hand, even if it's not a penalty situation, distracts from the run." (Sam Shepard)
- A "natural" rider: one who looks part of the horse instead of sitting stiffly or standing in the stirrups.
- A rider who recognizes when he has cut a dull cow and quits it early so that he can spend time working a better one.
- A good showman. "You pay more attention when you see a showman out there." (Todd Williamson) A showman has composure. He works the herd and doesn't hurry or force mistakes. He makes clean, decisive cuts. He goes for broke at just the right moments. He is aware of the time left on the clock, and will not spend time hiding in the herd. "People who are winning are good showmen. They can bring up a score a half a point. I'm a stickler for good showmanship." (Tim Smith)

What a Judge
Likes *to See in a Run*

- Good herdwork. Smooth, pretty cuts on a loose rein: The rider goes after the cow he wants to cut, brings her up through the herd, and makes a clean, centered cut. "It's hard to mark a run high without pretty herdwork. For example, taking the last cow instead of cutting one out, is not a point-earning situation. To visibly cut a cow: that's what it's all about." (Joe Jones)

- A group of cattle that is driven far enough up the arena to demonstrate the rider's ability to control them.
- A challenging run. "A judge has to adjust his judgment to go with the cattle being worked and to what's going on out there. If a horse is really tried by a cow and, as a result, is on the border of being out of position, it's almost to his credit. Some judges may disagree and go strictly by what's in the book, but tougher situations call for tougher, less correct moves." (Brent Layton)
- A run where horse and rider break down a tough cow so that she can be controlled in the center of the pen.
- Tough cattle being worked. "I want to see you take a chance and cut a tough cow. I don't want to see two-and-a-half minutes of watching paint dry; I want to see something happening." (Tim Smith)
- Quitting with both style and intent to turn around and find another good cow to work.

What the Judges Suggest

- Attend an NCHA Judges' Seminar or special clinic for applicants. "Many people who are showing today, even some of the best, do not know the rules. You should go to a Judges' Seminar to learn what a judge is being taught to look for." (Rod Edwards)
- Analyze several runs with a judge so that you can understand his viewpoint and learn how he arrives at a score.
- Learn to be a showman. "If you have a questionable quit or a miss, don't let the judge think you've made a mistake. Don't quit showing your horse, because you never know what things look like from the judge's seat." (Tim Smith)
- "Try to beat the *Rule Book*, not the guy who just had a great run." (Todd Williamson)
- "Cutting is a mind game. It's why we're in it. To stay cool under pressure seems to be the difference between the champions and the also-rans." (Joe Jones)
- "What helped my showing most was becoming a judge. You become more conscious of the little mistakes that detract from the appearance of a run." (Sam Shepard)
- Learn to read cattle so that you can pick one, separate it from the herd, and control it on your own.

In larger competitions, you will show under several judges. The final score reflects the combined opinions of these officials. However, when you choose to show under only one judge, usually the case at smaller competitions, you assume the risk that he might miss something in your turn which could affect the final score, and also that he may have certain prejudices that are either to your advantage or disadvantage. The judge is human, don't forget. But also realize that he *wants* to judge; that he will do his best to mark every run in an unbiased manner and to abide by the current NCHA *Rule Book.*

15

PSYCHOLOGY AND SHOWMANSHIP: THE ART OF WINNING

Don't ever tip your hand to the judge

–LINDY BURCH

Success comes from proper training, experience in the show ring, and figuring out how to gain the upper hand on your fellow cutters. Many technically correct trainers and nonpros with excellent horses are beatable if you can bring something more to the party. That something is a combination of psychology and showmanship.

Mental preparation for competition begins at home. It requires a solid foundation: knowing your horse's capabilities as well as your own, and then taking those factors into the competitive arena.

Mike Haack on Dox Royal Hickory (*courtesy:* NCHA).

To earn a very high score of 76, you need to do something special. You've often got to be on the verge of a wreck, to hang it out there and make the judge sit up and take notice of you. You have to create a unique presentation and use some theatrics to get him behind you. Nowadays, winning a cutting competition is more than technical. It's an act—a class act.

By now, you've ridden enough that your reactions come without thinking. You have some confidence in your abilities and can put more effort into learning the finer points of showing. Watch top riders more closely, and study those who really look good in front of a judge. These riders create their own luck. They exude confidence because they know their horses' capabilities. They spend plenty of time figuring out a strategy that will show a horse's strengths and cover up his weaknesses. This sets them apart mentally from most of their competition.

But you can still beat them, and presentation is the key. From the moment you enter the arena you need to be a showman. Enter believing in what you are doing. Look confident, prepared, relaxed, and focused. Project these qualities to a judge who has had pressure on him all day long, and he'll

Joe Heim riding the Triple Crown winner Doc's Okie Quixote.

sit up and take notice. He'll find it more difficult to spot errors if you are doing everything in your power to make your run appear flawless.

A good way to understand the importance of showmanship is to look at competition from the judge's seat. He may have been sitting for a long period of time, trying hard to concentrate. Then in comes another rider. The horse looks good to the judge, but so do lots of other horses that he has been watching. When entering the herd, the rider seems fairly uncomfortable (the judge makes a mental note), and his helpers are doing much of the work. Although he keeps looking at a particular cow as though he may want to cut her (mental note), the rider winds up with another cow (another mental note). After a couple of turns, the cow runs across the pen and the rider leans in toward her, acting as if his horse should have turned (mental note) earlier. The next pass is correct, but then the cow becomes tougher and "tries" the horse hard on one side. Instead of becoming just as tough, the rider pulls up to quit when the cow turns away. He appears to be rattled (mental note).

This cutter has been out there perhaps only one minute so far, yet he has already created a negative impression. While he walks back to the herd, the judge is thinking: "Must be pretty new at this . . . Doesn't look very confident . . . Didn't even get close to cutting that cow he was watching . . . Was he leaning because his horse was a little bit late in that turn? . . . He wasn't too happy about that quit . . . Did I miss something?" The judge isn't taking points away here, he's just thinking about things, and wondering how many more riders are in this class, and who's up next. Maybe it'll be someone with a little bit of flair . . . .

This kind of performance is an example of a cutter who does not have a positive attitude and has no idea of how to appear in control. If he were a better showman, he could hide his indecision and errors in judgment, leaving the judge with a better impression.

My husband, a bicycle racer, came home two years ago from a tough series of races in Europe. He looked thin, but felt good and was ready for more. We talked about how different people mentally prepare themselves for competition, and about success and failure. He said that bicycle racers fall into two categories: those who are quiet and focused, and those who expend a lot of energy making excuses and complaining. He felt that many of his fellow riders were looking for a reason to lose.

Cutting is no different. The next time you're at a show, listen to the banter between the judge's stand and count the times you hear complaints about the pen, the ground, the cattle, the dust, the judge, the draw, the horse, the nerves, or the help. I'm just as guilty whenever I feel unsure of myself and want something to blame when I lose. And I want an excuse right there, handy, when the buzzer sounds. But this happens less now because I love the sport so much and I know that when I work hard I can do well. I've developed a process of knowing more, and understanding that there are going to be good days when I do well and bad days when nothing seems to work.

Performance and Attitude

Your performance in competition is the result of a network of variables. Some of these variables are controllable, and some simply are not. The trick is to come to terms with the areas that are beyond your control and somehow make peace with them. Realize that you cannot control the noise, the footing, the lighting, the time factor, what the judge is thinking, what bunch of cattle you are in, or when you'll work. You can't control who will be your competition on a particular day, or which cattle they will choose to work, or when they will work. Leave these things behind. Don't spend your energy thinking and worrying about them: They are negatives, and they'll drain you.

Bill Freeman on Smart Little Lena (*courtesy:* NCHA).

Heading down the road for a show very early one morning, I had settled into my own little world when the red trouble light flickered on the dashboard. Fortunately, I was near a small town. After pacing around and fretting until the gas station opened at 6:00 A.M., I had worked myself into a pretty good lather and was barely able to avoid full drama while the attendant slowly looked things over. It would take at least an hour. And I would miss my first class.

I spent far too much energy during that hour. I worried about missing the show, about the prepaid entry fee, about my horse, about the oil filter, and on and on. The attendant noticed my anxiety level (which wasn't hard), and finally remarked, "Lady, I'd like to give you a little advice that would maybe help. We can't do anything to make the oil filter arrive here sooner. We can't control this. So it's really not a problem you should be worrying about."

But what *can* you influence? You can control your own decisions: how to train, how to ride, which horse to bring, which classes to enter, how to warm up, whom you choose to help, which cattle you cut, and how you perform. Most of these "controllables" are deeply rooted in the months of preparation

Buster Welch working cattle from what he calls "The best seat in the house."

you've done at home. Your responses should be fairly automatic by the time you arrive at the showgrounds. But if they aren't, don't be self-critical or judgmental. Turn it into a learning experience.

You can also influence the way you think. A good example is in the way you perceive your heroes. Successful cutters will put the pressure on you—if you let them. You know that they have spent a lot more hours in the saddle, and they have a confident look. But they're human too. They are just as uneasy as you are, making demands upon themselves and struggling with anxiety. If you have done your training and are committed to giving total effort to the moment, you'll be able to hold your own out there. You *can* compete against your heroes, but only if you believe in yourself and try your hardest. After all, doing your best is all that really counts.

When you ride into an arena, ride with the attitude that you have a good horse and you're there to show him off. Don't frustrate yourself with negative thoughts that can undermine your performance. Those two and a half minutes of work are yours alone, so be there 100 percent without dwelling on mistakes or successes. The reason you practice is to get familiar with every possible situation and work through it. You can try for a good run, but you can't *make* it happen. Let success come from confidence in knowing the simplicity of cutting, from making your nerves work as adrenaline for you, and from savoring your time doing what you like to do.

Two examples of positive attitude are Buster Welch and Chubby Turner. Both men, who "live and breathe" cutting horses, are successful because of their attitudes toward the sport. Buster says he figured out long ago that "cutting competition is nothing more than a contest of 'oh shits' and 'attaboys.' And the person with more 'attaboys' is the winner." Chubby will begin one of his excellent clinics by saying, "Never forget that the basic principles of cutting are left–stop–right–stop. You've got a cow with no brains just trying to get back to the herd, and all you have to do is stay even with her."

The cutters who pick up checks at most competitions are showmen. The points below have been gathered from some of these riders, as well as from clinics given by Chubby Turner, Lindy Burch, Mike Haack, and Bill Freeman. Practice them at home so that they become as natural to you as your other reactions.

Entering the herd. Exude confidence and be direct in your approach when walking toward the herd. Look as though you are eager to show an excellent horse to the judge, and that you know how to do it. When you enter the herd, it looks more professional to keep your hand low and quiet and to use your legs more than your reins when guiding your horse—you'll appear in full control of a calm horse.

Show the judge that you are thinking about some particular cattle, and that you have a plan in mind to shape them toward the front of the herd. Let him know you're not just standing there wasting time while your helpers do the work.

Driving. There are many subtle things you can do with your horse when driving cattle up the middle of the arena. For example, if your horse feels "chargy," you might drive a comfortable distance and then lift your rein slightly to back him up a step. This tells him to wait for you. As long as your horse responds, you can subtly make a very strong point.

Shaping. When shaping the herd, try to avoid the bad cattle and set up the good ones. If you're shaping one that is out in front, but then another cow suddenly takes over, act as though that cow is the one you intended to shape all along. Don't show panic, and don't let the judge know you miscalculated and couldn't get the cow you wanted.

Leon Harrel and Todd Bimat are very good at this kind of showmanship. A judge will never know what Leon is thinking when he's out there in the herd (even if his helpers do). Todd is one who never has tunnel vision. He's good at surveying the whole scene while actually testing a cow he likes that is in the middle.

At a clinic devoted entirely to showmanship, Chubby Turner stressed going into the arena with the idea of making it tough for the judge to find errors in your work. You might be the first person the judge sees that day, or the hundredth, but never allow him to pick up on a mistake by showing him you are making one. In other words, don't wave any red flags when you're out there in the middle of the arena.

Setting up for a cut. Your ability to select cows that will suit your horse has much to do with the way he will show. Don't choose a high-headed, wild cow for a tentative horse or young colt. And don't cut a big, slow cow for a horse that can hold his own on something with spark. When you feel that one cow will work for you, and she's still in the herd, step to her shoulder while you're looking around at the others. If she responds to you, try to shape her toward the middle of the pen.

While you are shaping and getting set up to make your cut, remind your horse that you mean business and that he'd better listen. You can do so without risking penalty points as long as you are subtle. While looking at cows and shaping one that is still in the herd, ask your horse to step to the right or left by using your leg. Then sit down deeper in the saddle and lift up slightly on the reins. Let him know he has to move off your leg and then stop. Your timing must be near perfect as you do this so that the judge doesn't take notice of any schooling. Use rein and leg only when you would naturally step left or right to stop a cow or control the herd's direction.

Making the cut. Don't be too hasty when choosing a cow to work, but be definite about it once you've decided. Let the judge know that you had a certain cow in mind and you were able to get her, even if it isn't true.

Next, establish your horse's balance on the cow. The way he begins his work is most important. Don't turn him loose until you are absolutely certain he's hooked to that cow and will stay correct. If you need to reestablish those left and right boundaries for him, do it quickly and with finesse by checking him on either side before letting him work on his own. Doing so may cost you a point or two if the judge notices, but you'll earn those points back twofold with a correct and centered run.

There is another way to school your horse before turning him loose to work a cow. If, for instance, he doesn't break off well going to the right, or if he feels too pushy when moving in that direction, you can establish that first right turn for him without penalty by using your leg. Ask your horse to step toward the cow in a way that will cause your horse to turn right. Make him exaggerate this right turn by pressing your left spur into his side. You haven't done anything illegal, yet you've made your point.

The work. What separates the really good works from the average is showmanship and an ability to recover from mistakes. This is where timing and practice come into play.

When novice riders make mistakes (or what Buster calls an "oh shit"), they tend to dwell on them for the next few turns. This causes a loss of timing, which in turn leads to being late, which leads to the judge deducting points from the work. The same is true in the case of a horse doing something good (an "attaboy"). The rider might think, "Wow, what a turn. My horse was right in the ground." You'll again be late. So avoid dwelling on errors and resting on your laurels. Focus only on what is ahead, and get cookin' again. Know that each stop and turn must be in balance with the cow—you've got to be in tune if you want to dance with your partner.

Part of putting on a good performance is projecting yourself in the image you want to be, and then sticking to it. You'll have that confident look that may pull you through a tough situation even if your run is less than perfect. You can learn this confidence by spending a lot of time in the saddle, and by figuring out ways to get out of almost every predicament. Watch some of the top pros and nonpros ride, and you'll see good examples of how to gloss over errors that could otherwise cost half a point or more. Jolene Nelson, for instance, never looks rattled even when she's having a hard time. She can make a bad situation look good just by appearing confident and under control.

A judge wants to see a cutter who gives a run 100 percent. This kind of intensity is contagious. If you are doing a good job, and are fully involved in cutting and holding your cow, the judge will begin to pull for you. He might start watching the cow with such intensity that he misses an error you made.

Quitting. The way you quit working a cow will help cement the judge's impression of your entire work. Be definite about it, leaving no question of your intention. Look at that cow as though you have put her where you want her and are ready to move on. Again, it's a matter of theatrics. You don't have to shoot the lights out with a run chock full of "attaboys" to win. You may not even feel good about your whole performance, but it's what the judge thinks that counts.

There will be many times when you do something a bit questionable when quitting, and times when both you and the fence sitters know that you committed a major error. But don't give the judge any hint of what you're thinking because he just may have gone to sleep for a second and missed your error. Here are a few examples:

- You might pick up on the reins just a split second too late, or quit when the cow's not obviously turned away from you. Look hard at that cow in a definite way, as if you've really fixed her. Then go back and cut another. Chubby Turner calls this ploy the "John Wayne look" (Lindy Burch calls it the "Chubby Turner look").
- Quitting at the very side of the arena doesn't look good, but sometimes you have no choice. Your horse might be winded, or you may feel you will lose the cow if you try to hold her any longer. Another good reason to pull up at the side fence is when you think your horse is going to quit on you. Whatever your reason, make it positive. Stop, then turn around toward the center before going back to the herd. In that way, you will bring the judge's attention right back to the middle.
- If you've cut a bad cow, look for a place to quit after a few turns so you can get another cow and show the judge your horse's ability. But, again, keep it positive. Don't let on that you're trying to find a good place to quit.

My husband gave me some good advice about showmanship and attitude just before I went to my first series of futurities. He said, "Drive it like you own it." Your thoughts can dictate your performance. A show can be a positive experience only if you believe it. You're not going to win first every time. And you're going to go to at least one cutting where the judge kills you, and to another where he gifts you. But everything evens out. Each time, you start with a clean sheet of paper. Each time, you must walk into that arena like a pro and leave it like one.

When It's Over

Cutting competition has been compared to basketball, poker, pool, bicycle racing, and pulling the lever on a slot machine. It takes a perfect combination

Time to relax during a change of cattle at the B Bar B Cutting in Idaho. (*photo:* **Paul Holmes**)

of skill, finesse, offensive and defensive maneuvering, as well as a little luck to be a winner. And because these different pieces don't always fall together just right in a short two-and-a-half-minute run, nobody is able to dominate the cutting world with consistent wins. Each show brings a new opportunity for each person to get out and do well. If you *want* to improve and are willing to do your homework and set realistic goals for both yourself and your horse, you may find competition to be fairly addictive.

Last fall I was in Los Angeles for the Pacific Coast Futurities. My day hadn't gone well. The typical had happened: a case of nerves, thinking about an impending operation (successful), a bad draw in the last bunch of cattle, and the problem of my futurity horse losing an aluminum shoe that couldn't be matched. Carrying all this extra baggage with me, I went into the arena when my name was announced. Two and a half minutes later the buzzer sounded and I knew we wouldn't make the semis. Damn. If I'd only . . .

That evening I called home to relate the day's happenings to my husband and kids and say I'd be coming home earlier than anticipated. Behind me at the phone booth was a friend and fellow competitor, Dan Lufkin. When I hung up and turned around, he just smiled warmly and said, "Don't forget, Lynn, this is what makes us all come back." It really *is* like pulling the lever on a slot machine.

Cutting is a game. It's a new game every time you walk into a herd of cattle. It can be humbling, but it cannot make or break you. Be a student of the sport. Do your best to come out on top, and perform as well as you can under the circumstances. There will be times when you know you were gifted by the judge, and other times when you feel cheated. But these even out in the long run. Overlook them and move forward.

APPENDIX A

2000 NCHA Rules for
Judging Cutting Horse Contents

1. Each horse is required to enter the herd sufficiently deep enough to show his ability to make a cut. One such deep cut will satisfy this rule. Failure to satisfy this requirement will result in a three (3) point penalty.

    a. A horse will be rewarded credit for his ability to enter the herd quietly with very little disturbance to the herd or to the one brought out.

2. When an animal is cut from the herd, it is more desirable that it be taken toward the center of the arena, and credit will be rewarded for same. Additional credit will be rewarded to the horse which drives its stock sufficient distance from the herd to assure that the herd will not be disturbed by his work; thereby showing his ability to drive a cow.

3. Credit will be recognized for riding with a loose rein throughout a performance.

4. Credit will be recognized for setting up a cow and holding it in a working position as near the center of the arena as possible.

5. If the cutting horse or his rider creates disturbance at any time throughout his working period, he will be penalized:

    a. Any noise directed by the contestant toward the cattle will be penalized one (1) point.

    b. Each time a horse runs into the herd, scatters the herd while working, or picks up cattle through fault of the horse, he will be penalized three (3) points.

    c. The judge shall stop any work because of training or abuse of his horse by the contestant or disturbance of the cattle. Any contestant failing to stop immediately will be fined $500.00 payable to NCHA prior to entry in any other NCHA approved event.

6. A horse will be penalized three (3) points each time the back fence actually stops or turns the animal being worked within one step (three [3] feet) of the fence; the back fence to be agreed on and designated by the judge or judges before the contest starts; meaning the actual fence only, no imaginary line from point to point to be considered. If any of the contestants voices an objection before the contest starts, the judge or judges shall take a vote of the contestants, and a "back fence" acceptable to the majority shall be designated and used.

7. If a horse turns the wrong way with tail toward the animal being worked, an automatic score of sixty (60) points will be given.

8. While working, a horse will be penalized one (1) point each time the reins are used to control or direct (to rein) the horse, regardless of whether the reins are held high or low. A one (1) point penalty shall also be charged whenever a horse is visibly cued in any manner. If the reins are tight enough that the bits are bumped at any time, he shall be penalized one (1) point each time even though the hand of the rider does not move.

    a. A horse must be released as soon as the desired animal is clear of the other cattle. Additional reining, cuing or positioning will result in a one (1) point penalty for each occurrence.

    b. The rider shall hold the bridle reins in one hand. A three (3) point penalty shall be charged if the second hand touches the reins for any purpose except to straighten them.

    c. Spurring behind the shoulder shall not be considered a visible cue. A three (3) point penalty shall be assessed each time a horse is spurred in the shoulder.

    d. A toe, foot, or stirrup on the horse's shoulder is considered a visible cue. A one (1) point penalty shall be charged for each occurrence.

9. If a horse lets an animal that he is working get back in the herd, he will be penalized five (5) points.

10. If a rider changes cattle after visibly committing to a specific cow, a five (5) point penalty will be assessed.

11. When a horse goes past an animal to the degree he loses his working advantage, he will be penalized one (1) point each time he does so.

12. Unnecessary roughness, such as a horse actually pawing, biting, or kicking cattle,

will be penalized three (3) points.

13. A contestant may quit an animal when it is obviously stopped, obviously turned away, or is obviously behind the turnback horses and the turnback horses are behind the time line. A penalty of three (3) points must be charged if the animal is quit under any other circumstances.

14. If a horse quits a cow, a penalty of five (5) points will be assessed.

15. If a horse clears the herd with two (2) or more cattle and fails to separate a single animal before quitting, a five (5) point penalty will be charged. There is no penalty if time expires.

16. Horses must be ridden with a bridle having a bit in the mouth or with a hackamore. A bridle shall have no nose band or bosal, and hackamores shall be of rope or braided rawhide with no metal parts. A judge must be able to freely pass two fingers between the hackamore and muzzle completely around the horse's nose. Choke ropes, tie downs, wire around the horse's neck, nose, or brow band, tight nose band, quirt, bat, or mechanical device giving the rider undue control over a horse will not be permitted in the arena where an NCHA approved or sponsored event is being held. Wire of any kind and on any part of the curb device is not permissible. Breast collar may be used, no portion of which may pass over the horse's neck. Breast collars attached to the swell of the saddle on competing horses will be considered illegal. Chaps and spurs may be worn. A competing horse's tail cannot be tied in any manner which would restrict movement of the tail. Any time a contestant is guilty of an infraction of this rule or any part therein, he shall be disqualified. A judge has the right to have a contestant report to him if he is suspicious of any infraction of Rule 16.

    a. All riders must comply with Rule 16 when in any part of the arena.

    b. Any person in the arena after the start of an NCHA approved or sponsored event must wear western attire, including hats. The hat requirement may be waived at outdoor shows, both in and outside the working area of the arena, in extreme weather conditions with the consent of both Show Management and the judges(s). Men must wear long-sleeved shirts with collars and buttons or snaps completely down the shirt front. T-shirts and slipover knits are not permissible. Women must wear long-sleeved shirts with a collar. Sweaters may be worn over an appropriate shirt. Long sleeves must be worn rolled down. In extreme weather, show management, with the consent of the judge, may also allow deviation from the dress requirements with regard to hats and/or sleeve length at outdoor shows both in and outside the working area of the arena.

c. Rule 16 shall become effective one (1) hour prior to the published starting time of championship and jackpot cuttings. At limited age events and other special events approved by the NCHA, Rule 16 shall become effective three (3) hours prior to the published starting time each day and shall remain in effect until one hour after each day's performance is concluded.

d. Rule 16 may be set aside by show management for an official practice session provided that the practice session ends at least one hour prior to the start of any performance.

e. Contestants are limited to a maximum of four (4) helpers.

f. If an Officer, Director, or duly elected or appointed contestant's representative of the NCHA witnesses a violation of Standing Rule 16, they must report the violation immediately to the Association Executive Director.

g. Violations of Rule 16, Subsections (b) or (c), shall result in:

    i. First offense—$200.00 fine.

    ii. Second offense—$500.00 fine.

    iii. Third and subsequent offenses within 12 months—90 day suspension.

h. Any member seeking approval to use an electronic hearing device during an NCHA approved contest must meet or exceed the minimum criteria for hearing impairment, based on the results of an audiogram administered by a licensed physician.

    i. An application to use an electronic hearing devise must be submitted to NCHA, along with the member's audiogram results.

    ii. The transmitter of the device must be one of the contestant's four (4) helpers.

    iii. The user of an electronic hearing device can be required to be tested by an NCHA appointed physician if a complaint or protest arises in connection with the user's degree of hearing impairment.

17. When a contestant is thrown from a horse or a horse falls to ground, an automatic score of sixty (60) points will be given.

18. Any rider who allows his horse to quit working or leaves the working arena before his allotted time is up will be disqualified for that go-round with no score.

19. A contestant will be awarded a complete rework if in the judge or judges' opinior two and one-half (2^1/2) minutes time was not allotted for the work or if excessive disturbances had been created by factors other than those caused by the contestant or his/her help and the judge or judges have stopped the time. Such factors would include gates coming open, fences falling down and objects entering or falling into the working portion of the arena, but would not apply to cattle scattering through wildness or normal arena activities. Any rework must take place within the group of cattle drawn by the contestant and must occur before a change of cattle is executed. At the contestant's option, the rework may occur immediately or as the last work in that set of cattle. No rework shall be granted if the contestant involved has incurred a three (3) or five (5) point (major) penalty prior to a disturbance. After the cutter has completed his two and one half-minutes work, if in his/her opinion a situation has occurred of sufficient seriousness so as to warrant a rerun, he may immediately make a request for the same to the Contestant's Representative or to the designated equipment judge who shall report this fact to show management before the next horse is called to work. Show management shall make such facts as are available known to the judge(s) and if the majority are in agreement that due cause did exist, a re-run may be granted provided the original work was free of a three (3) or a five (5) point (major) infraction. If the clock has not started, a re-work will automatically be granted.

20. A judge marks from sixty (60) to eighty (80) points. One-half (1/2) points are permissible.

21. When the judge is in doubt about a penalty, the benefit always goes to the contestant.

[courtesy: NCHA]

Index for NCHA Judge's Card

Credits

Herdwork–Rule 1
Driving a cow–Rule 2
Loose reins–Rule 3
Setting up a cow–working center of arena–Rule 4

Penalties

1 point–(miss) losing working advantage—Rule 11
1 point–reined or visibly cued positioning after cut in clear—Rule 8
1 point–toe, foot, or stirrup on horse's shoulder—Rule 8d
1 point–noise directed to cattle—Rule 5a
3 points–cattle picked up running into or scattered herd—Rule 5b
3 points–failure to make a deep cut—Rule 1a
3 points–hot quit—Rule 13
3 points–pawing or biting cattle—Rule 12
3 points–second hand on reins while cutting or working—Rule 8b
3 points–spurring in shoulder—Rule 8c
3 points–backfence—Rule 6
5 points–horse quitting cow—Rule 14
5 points–changing cattle after specific commitment—Rule 10
5 points–failure to separate a single animal after leaving the herd—Rule 15
60 score–horse turns tail—Rule 7
60 score–horse falls to ground—Rule 17
Disqualification from go-round—leaving working area before time expires—Rule 18
Disqualification from contest—illegal equipment—Rule 16 (also Standing Rule 38)

(courtesy: NCHA)

APPENDIX C

NCHA JUDGES CARD

Event _____

Go Round _____

RUN CONTENT:

Herd Work
Driving a Cow
Setting Up a Cow
Loose Reins
Working Center of Arena
Degree of Difficulty
Amount of Courage
Time Worked +/-
Excessive Herdholder Help

PENALTIES:

(a) 1 point - (miss) losing working advantage (11)
(b) 1 point - reined or visibly cued (8)
(c) 1 point - noise directed to cattle (5a)
(d) 1 point - toe, foot or stirrup on the shoulder (8d)

(a) 3 points - hot quit (13)
(b) 3 points - cattle picked up or scattered (5b)
(c) 3 points - second hand on reins (8b)
(d) 3 points - spur in shoulder (8c)
(e) 3 points - pawing or biting cattle (12)
(f) 3 points - failure to make a deep cut (1)
(g) 3 points - back fence (6)

(a) 5 points - horse quitting a cow (14)
(b) 5 points - losing a cow (9)
(c) 5 points - changing cattle after a specific commitment (10)
(d) 5 points - failure to separate a single animal after leaving the herd (15)

60 - if horse turns tail (7)
60 - if horse falls to ground (17)

Disqualification (score 0) - illegal equipment, or leaves working area before time expires

HORSE	SCORE	PENALTIES			RUN CONTENT						
		1 PT	3 PTS	5 PTS	Herd Work	Setting Up a Cow	Degree of Difficulty	Eye Appeal	Time Working	✓ Excessive Herdholder Help	

+ Above Average
✓ Average
- Below Average

Judge's Signature _____

176

APPENDIX D

Troubleshooting

When a problem arises during training or showing, you should *feel* it immediately. You should be tuned in to your horse so that you can recognize an error and then figure out *why* it occurred. The result is a better understanding of what to do to make things right.

Most trainers will first look to you, the rider, when a horse does something wrong. Were you focused on the cow and decisive in your movements? Were your reins too tight? Was your body twisted or stiff? Were your legs or spurs inadvertently hitting the horse? Did you give the wrong signal? Did he understand what you asked of him? Then, they will think about the horse and the situation he was in when he erred. Was he pushed to do more than he was capable of? Was he frightened? Is something wrong with him? Should he know better?

The following are common mistakes that trainers see in horses (and riders), and suggestions for fixing these problems.

The Horse

Hops or dances in front of a cow. This may be the result of pushing a horse to do too much too quickly in training. Let him think for himself. Don't ask him to do any more than the cow is doing.

Wants to commit too early to a cow. This means that you haven't controlled him. Don't let him be too fresh. Make him wait for you on a loose rein. You should be able to have *contact* with the bit at a moment's notice.

Is short on cow. If your horse is late when moving across the pen with a cow, he probably will be long when going the other way. Even him up so that you have *balance* during the entire work. Also, be sure that he does not lose the cow when he's late, even if you have to go to the back fence to hold the cow.

Stops long. This may be caused by you, so be sure you help your horse stop by sitting down in the saddle and staying out of his sides with your legs. If he is still long, he will be short on the cow when she turns the other way. Ride hard to catch up, and he will probably correct himself. Or, stop and back him up over his tracks when he is long, press him in the other direction, and then make him catch up with the cow. Another method is to let him stop and turn on his own, then stop him hard before catching up to the cow. Also, whenever you use your horse to make a cow move, be sure to drive toward the hip of the cow, not the head.

Stops short. Get your timing down. Don't allow him to stop any earlier than when is correct. Exaggerate the correct position by pushing him a little long on a soft cow. Build his confidence. Show him that he can still control this cow if he stops long.

Doesn't stop crisply. Quickly back him a few steps each time he stops.

Ignores you when you ask him to stop or back up. If he's a colt, lighten up his mouth by using a twisted wire snaffle for a week. If he is older, back him up over his tracks every time you ask for a stop.

Doesn't pay attention to the cow when he stops. Use your cow-side hand on the reins when you stop. This will keep his nose tipped in toward the cow so that he can see her and learn to read her.

Twists his head toward the cow too much. As a result of this behavior, he may drop his shoulder toward the cow or dive in toward her. Even him out by using your herd-side hand on the reins or by holding the reins independently. Let him tell you how much correcting he needs.

Stops early and wants to turn in toward the cow. Let him make this mistake and then show him why he shouldn't do it. Ride him toward the cow if this is what he wants to do. When she moves, make him turn hard and get over to where he should be. He'll soon discover that he has to work harder whenever he wants to move toward a cow.

Cheats by turning in on the ends. Don't ever let him learn that he can scare a cow by turning in toward her, and don't allow a mediocre stop. Shorten up your reins and ride with your herd-side hand on them at all times. Set him in the ground when he stops and then leave him alone. If he then tries to turn in, back him up a few steps and then make him go forward parallel to the cow again.

Jumps out toward the cow. This probably means that your horse has learned he can keep a cow away from the herd by scaring her. Take him in a long arena and drive a few cows to the far end before making a cut. Then exaggerate each turn he makes by pressing him with your leg. Make him fade back toward the herd. Also, use your reins to check him quickly when you feel him start to come out.

Rushes the turns. Stop earlier and stop correctly so that he doesn't have a chance to turn in toward the cow.

Turns too slowly. A horse that doesn't have those crisp, hard turns probably lacks a good stop. Put down the foundation before you expect the results.

Makes barrel turns. Often caused by the rider. Be sure your legs are not stiff or gripping his sides, and that your body isn't twisted or leaning toward the cow in anticipation of a turn. A horse that wants to turn in toward a cow on the ends is a horse that has never learned to stop correctly. Get your timing down. Think in terms of what Bill Freeman calls "riding for the stop." Don't even think about turning, because it will happen naturally if your horse is "cowing." Then all you should do is to help him finish his turn if he needs it.

Leaking. If your horse comes out *toward* a cow at any time during his work, either when turning or when moving across the pen, he is losing his working advantage. A "barrel" turn (or rounded turn) will not allow him adequate time to stay even with a fast-turning cow. And if he comes out toward the cow on his turn, he has lessened his chances of holding her out there and preventing her return to the herd.

Check to make sure that you are not stiff or gripping him tightly with your legs. If he still comes out toward the cow he's working, do more driving. Use either the round or square pen to drive cattle out far. After making your cut, break him hard to the right and left with your spur. Then leave him alone and let him think about it. Hopefully, the cow will teach him why he should stay back and protect himself from her attack. If you can't find an aggressive cow, ask a helper to push any cow straight toward your horse. Make him learn to be cautious regardless of what the rider is doing.

Fades back too far. If your horse has learned to fade backwards, it may be because you have allowed him to be late (and behind) on the cow he is working. Control the degree of his turn so that he makes less than a complete turn each time. And don't allow him to be late when he initiates his turn.

Breaks harder to the left. You are probably getting one-sided on him, using your right leg harder and dragging his head over with your left hand. Use only your right hand on the reins for a while, and concentrate on being physically and mentally balanced. And practice turning in the direction in which he is weak. Walk him up to the cow's hip to begin the turn, and then use your spur to put him in the right position when she moves.

Does not break hard when turning. Use your leg (and spur) to finish each turn. Practice against a flat section of fence so that you can make sure he finishes each turn.

Runs off on one side. Try to figure out why. Is it something that may have happened in earlier training to scare him? Can it be remedied by tipping his nose toward the cow and working in a less pressured situation? Try some reverse psychology: Encourage him to run off, but then *make* him get back to the cow by putting a lot of pressure on him.

Flips his head. The bit might hurt, or there may be a problem with his teeth. If this is just a bad habit left over from his past, get more leverage on his head by holding the reins much farther up toward his mouth (midneck). This way, as soon as he tries to throw his head, see-saw on the reins and do not allow him any upward movement. You must be ready to do this *before* it happens.

Overreacts to the cow. Slow down and don't keep pressuring him. Concentrate on making only the movements necessary to stay correct with the cow.

Walks away from cow being worked. Drive him to the cow. Make him watch the cow and take responsibility for her.

Is too pushy. Keep your hands down low and wait for him to make a mistake. Then hurt him for it by backing him up hard. Leave him alone again by staying light with your hands until he gives you another reason to correct him.

APPENDIX E

Glossary

Alligator. A very tough cow that does not respect a horse and will do anything to get back to the herd.

Back Fence. The fence that is directly behind the herd. A cow being worked must not be allowed to reach any portion of the back fence. (Refer to the NCHA *Rule Book* for specifics and penalty points regarding the back fence.)

Balanced. Working a cow evenly, mirroring her movements and preventing her from having any advantage over your horse.

Break off. To move a horse quickly to one side with your leg or spur.

Bubble. The area or space that surrounds a cow. By positioning your horse near the edge of a cow's bubble, you can influence her speed and direction.

Bump. The quick application and release of your spur against a horse's belly or shoulder; a way to get his attention without hurting or scaring him.

Bump the bit. To pull back with one or both reins just enough to make the horse feel and react to the bit. A rider can inadvertently bump the bit and confuse his horse when the reins are uneven or when he holds them too tight.

Bump a cow. To move a cow by getting closer to her.

Centered work. Controlling a cow so that she is trapped in the center portion of the arena when she is being worked.

Check. To pull back on the reins just enough to cause a horse to pause in his forward movement.

Collected. Describes a horse that is gathered up underneath himself and is balanced so that he can quickly respond to the moves of a cow.

Committing. When a rider takes visible action choosing a cow to cut, he is obligated to work that cow once he has *committed* to her.

Cowing. Describes a horse that is concentrating and focused on the cow in front of him.

Cow-side leg or hand. The leg or hand that is closer to the cow being worked.

Draw. To encourage a cow to come in toward you and your horse instead of scaring her away. This is a manipulative move in which you are positioned in such a way as to trick her into thinking she has a chance of returning safely to the herd.

Drive. To push a group of cattle forward in a controlled manner.

Dry work. Training done without the use of cattle. A cutting horse learns the basics of movement and how to respond to his rider during the dry work. From then on, most of his learning is the result of working and responding to a cow.

Flex. The ability of a horse to become supple by bending his body and neck in response to the rider's leg or rein.

Fresh. Describes a horse that has not been adequately warmed up before he is asked to work a cow. If he is fresh, he is not listening to you and not concentrating fully on his work.

Green-broke. A term referring to the minimum degree that a colt has been trained to respond to a rider.

Heading a cow. Going ahead of a cow in order to stop her or force her to change direction.

Herd-side leg or hand. The leg or hand that is closer to the herd of cattle.

Hooked. Refers to a horse that has his complete attention focused on the cow in front of him.

Leak. The action of a horse, during or after a turn, that causes him to come out toward the cow he is working instead of staying back. When a horse *leaks*, he often loses his working advantage over the cow.

Legged-up. The term applying to a horse that knows how to respond to his rider's leg. Also refers to a horse in fit condition.

Long. Being in an incorrect position on a cow being worked. If a horse moves ahead of a cow instead of remaining across from her shoulder or head, he will be *long*, and the cow will have the advantage.

Out of position. When a horse is unable to respond quickly enough to keep control over the cow he is working. He will lose his working advantage over the cow.

Peeling. Cattle in the center of an arena moving single file around the cutter and back toward the herd at the fence.

Pockets. The back pockets on a pair of jeans. When you sit a cutting saddle correctly, your pelvis is tilted back to the point where you almost literally sit on your rear pockets.

Press. To push leg or spur against an area of a horse's belly in order to get him to respond.

Quit. To stop working a cow. The rider signals his horse to quit by sitting down deep in the saddle and slightly lifting up the reins.

Rate. To stay in the correct position parallel with a moving cow.

Reading the cow. Anticipating the movements of a cow.

Rolling. Cattle that have been brought away from the main part of the herd become uncomfortable at a certain point because they want to go back to their buddies. Rolling is the term used to describe the way they begin to turn around and head for the herd. A roll can happen quite fast, and the rider must be ready to step forward to make a cut.

Schooling. Training; interceding when a horse is working improperly on his own.

Set up. To manipulate a cow so that she moves into the position you want her to be in order to separate her from the herd.

Settle. To help cattle become comfortable in one area, and to accustom them to a horse moving back and forth in front of them.

Shape. To manipulate cattle so that the best ones move in the direction you want them to go, while the wild or sour ones return to the main herd at the fence.

Short. Being behind and out of position on a cow when you are rating her. If you are short, you cannot control a cow's movement or direction.

Sort. To look over cattle and divide them according to your needs and their health.

Sour cattle. Cattle becomes less and less responsive to a horse when they are worked more than a few times. They will get to the point either where they refuse to move, or where they pay no attention to a horse.

Sticky. Describes cattle that are difficult to separate from one another.

Trail. To be short and out of position on a cow.

Tune. To sharpen up a horse's reaction time by insisting on perfect stops, tight turns, and accurate position on a cow.

Turning tail. When a horse turns away from the cow he is working in such a manner as to point his tail to the cow. If he turns tail to a cow in competition, he will automatically receive a minimum score of 60.

APPENDIX F

Loping Pen Etiquette and Guidelines

- Stay to the inside if you want to go slow, stay to the outside if you want to go fast.

- Never stop in traffic. Stop and do dry work in an area with no traffic. Apply boots and groom in areas with no traffic.

- If you must tie your horse, tie him to something secure. Do not tie studs, kicking, or biting horses in the loping pen. Someone may tie another horse close to yours. Do not get upset if someone spanks your horse for kicking or biting.

- Riders must be in control of their horses at all times.

- Look before leaving or entering traffic. Yield to lopers.

- Do not exercise horses or season young horses when there is limited space in this loping area.

- Do not weave in and out of traffic without looking. Maintain constant speed and stay to inside when going slow to help avoid the need for other people to have to weave in and out of traffic.

- Change directions and maintain flow in one direction when asked. Always ask when you wish to change directions.

- Yield to tractor and be careful of pedestrians and other lopers wishing to exit or enter. Leave pen when asked by announcer.

- Try to maintain a good sense of humor. People may be tired and nervous. Be patient with newcomers and try to help them learn by referring them to these guidelines.

[courtesy: NCHA]

INDEX

187